photographing
Yellowstone
National Park

Where to Find Perfect Shots and How to Take Them

Gustav W. Verderber

Gustav W. Verderber

THE COUNTRYMAN PRESS
WOODSTOCK, VERMONT

For my family, Ruth, John, Tina, and Wolfi,
and for Cheryl,
whose love sustains me.

Text and most photographs copyright © 2007 by Gustav W. Verderber

First Edition

Library of Congress Cataloging-in-Publication Data has been applied for.

ISBN-13: 978-0-88150-769-0

Cover photograph of Castle Geyser and interior photographs by the author unless otherwise specified
Cover and interior design by Susan Livingston
Maps by Paul Woodward, © The Countryman Press

Published by The Countryman Press, P.O. Box 748, Woodstock, VT 05091
Distributed by W.W. Norton & Company, Inc., 500 Fifth Avenue, New York, NY 10110

Printed in China by R. R. Donnelley

10 9 8 7 6 5 4 3 2 1

Acknowledgments

Thanks to the Kodak Ambassador Program, in addition to experiencing and photographing the grandeur of Yellowstone, I was also privileged to enjoy the company of some of the most wonderful people I have ever met in my travels. These include the many visitors to Yellowstone who kept me company during my sojourn in the park. I especially would like to thank the following individuals for their friendship, insights, advice, and inspiration—and without whose support this book would not have been possible:

Ben Baggett • Don Chamberlin • Dale Evva Gelfand • Bob Greenburg • Jeff Henry
Jett Hitt • Kermit Hummel • Candace Kendall • Tom Knox • Harlan Kredit
Marilyn Ridings • Carol Shively • Dan Stebbins • Warren Taylor • Jennifer Thompson
Bob Wesselman • Wayne Wolfensberger • Mike Vanian • Jeff Vanuga

Gustav W. Verderber

Beehive Geyser and the Firehole River

Old Faithful steaming at sunrise

Contents

Introduction 7
Using This Book 17
How I Photograph Yellowstone
National Park 18

I. Mammoth Hot Springs 29
1. Roosevelt Arch 29
2. Bighorn Sheep
   Wildlife Management Area 29
3. Albright Visitors Center 30
4. Travertine Terraces 30
5. Upper Terrace Loop Road 31
6. New Blue Spring 31
7. Canary Spring .31
8. Orange Spring Mound 32
9. Old Gardiner Road 33
10. Blacktail Plateau 34
11. Blacktail Plateau Drive 34
12. Grand Loop Road 34
13. Swan Lake Flats 34
14. Willow Park 35
15. Sheepeater Cliff 35

II. Madison and Norris Junctions 37
16. Madison Information Station 38
17. Terrace Spring 39
18. Gibbon Falls .39
19. Artist Paint Pots 39
20. Norris Geyser Basin 40
21. Echinus Geyser 40
22. Steamboat Geyser 40
23. Roaring Mountain 41

III. Old Faithful and West Thumb 44
24. West Thumb Geyser Basin 44
25. Big Cone 46
26. Fishing Cone .46
27. Abyss Pool 47
28. Black Pool 47
29. Twin Geysers .47
30. Upper Geyser Basin 48
31. Midway Geyser Basin 48
32. Lower Geyser Basin 48

33. Kepler Cascades 48
34. Lone Star Geyser 48
35. Old Faithful Geyser 48
36. Beehive Geyser 50
37. Firehole River 50
38. Heart Spring .50
39. Lion Geyser 50
40. Grand Geyser .50
41. Castle Geyser .52
42. Riverside Geyser 53
43. Grotto Geyser 55
44. Morning Glory Pool 55
45. Old Faithful Inn 55
46. Biscuit Basin .56
47. Black Sand Basin 56
48. Grand Prismatic Spring 56
49. Fairy Falls 56
50. Firehole Lake Drive 58
51. Firehole Spring 58
52. White Dome Geyser 58
53. Great Fountain Geyser 58
54. Fountain Paint Pot Nature Trail 58

IV. Fishing Bridge District 59
55. Fishing Bridge 59
56. Hayden Valley 59
57. Alum Creek 59
58. Elk Creek 59
59. Trout Creek 59
60. Mud Volcano .63
61. Dragon's Mouth 63
62. Sulphur Caldron 63
63. LeHardy's Rapids 64
64. Pelican Valley 64
65. Lake Butte Overlook 66
66. Sylvan Pass 66
67. Yellowstone Lake Hotel 66
68. Gull Point Drive 66

V. Canyon 69
69. Grand Canyon of Yellowstone 69
70. Canyon Village 69
71. Artist Point Overlook 69

72. Lower Falls 69
73. Upper Falls 72
74. Uncle Tom's Overlook 72
75. Uncle Tom's Trail 72
76. South Rim Trail 72
77. Lookout Point 72
78. Red Rocks Point .73
79. North Rim Trail 73
80. Grandview Point .73
81. Inspiration Point .73
82. Cascade Overlook Trail 74
83. Brink of the Lower Falls 74
84. Brink of the Upper Falls 74
85. Cascade Lake Trail 74

86. Cascade Lake 74
87. Mount Washburn Trail 76
88. Mount Washburn .76
89. Chittenden Road .77
90. Otter Creek Picnic Area 77

VI. Tower-Roosevelt & the Lamar Valley .78
91. Dunraven Pass 78
92. Tower Fall 78
93. Hexagonal Columns 78
94. Calcite Springs Overlook 79
95. Trout Lake 83

Suggested Itineraries 85
Photographic Data .88

Welcome to Yellowstone

In 1871 the photographer William Henry Jackson accompanied the Hayden Expedition into Yellowstone to help document the area's remarkable thermal features, stunning landscapes, and herds of wildlife. Indeed, it was Jackson's photographs plus the paintings of Henry W. Elliot and Thomas Moran—also traveling with the expedition—that inspired the public and, ultimately, Congress to establish America's first national park. More than a century later, anyone visiting Yellowstone National Park is emulating the efforts of these artists to capture the grandeur of Yellowstone; whether we capture what we see in our mind's eye, on canvas, on film, or, nowadays, on a silicon chip, we are all striving to convey a bit of Yellowstone's magnificence to others. This book is intended for all who wish to behold Yellowstone in its best light.

At 2.2 million acres, Yellowstone National Park is a formidable area to visit let alone photograph, and I do not by any stretch suggest that this guide covers every draw and peak of the park. Yet though Yellowstone's size does present a challenge, it is more than compensated for when you realize that, owing to its vastness, even after over a century of visitors—who now number upwards of 3 million each year—any one of us can still experience unique natural moments within the park and produce truly original images. In fact, Yellowstone continues to surprise us with new discoveries. I know a park ranger whose hobby it is to discover new waterfalls within the park. Imagine: waterfalls! Clearly, the photographic possibilities of Yellowstone have not, and perhaps never will be, exhausted. May the light be with you.

Pelican on the Yellowstone River

Gustav W. Verderber

Overview

The map of Yellowstone National Park shows the Grand Loop Road (12) that connects the various park villages: Mammoth Hot Springs, Tower-Roosevelt, Canyon, Fishing Bridge, Grant, and Old Faithful. While not hosting a village of full-service facilities, the Madison/ Norris junctions are commonly and collectively regarded as a distinct region since they are both significantly distant from the adjacent villages and distinguished by their unique collection of interesting features—that is, types of wildlife, geology, and the like.

Five entrances lead into the park. Four of

Yellowstone National Park

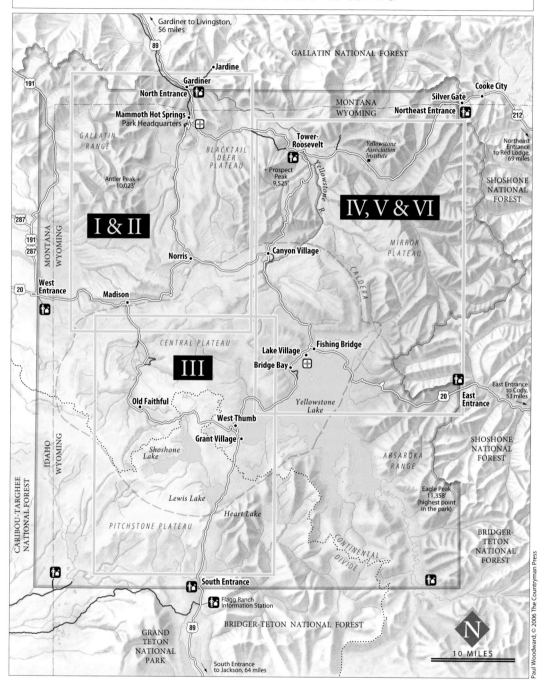

Gardiner to Livingston, 56 miles

GALLATIN NATIONAL FOREST

Jardine

Gardiner

North Entrance

Mammoth Hot Springs
Park Headquarters

MONTANA
WYOMING

Cooke City

Silver Gate

Northeast Entrance

GALLATIN RANGE

BLACKTAIL DEER PLATEAU

Tower-Roosevelt

Yellowstone Association Institute

Northeast Entrance to Red Lodge, 69 miles

SHOSHONE NATIONAL FOREST

Antler Peak + 10,023'

+ Prospect Peak 9,525'

I & II

IV, V & VI

MONTANA
WYOMING

Norris

Canyon Village

MIRROR PLATEAU

West Entrance

Madison

CENTRAL PLATEAU

Lake Village

Fishing Bridge

Bridge Bay

III

Old Faithful

West Thumb

Grant Village

Shoshone Lake

Yellowstone Lake

East Entrance to Cody, 53 miles

East Entrance

IDAHO
WYOMING

CARIBOU-TARGHEE NATIONAL FOREST

Lewis Lake

Heart Lake

PITCHSTONE PLATEAU

ABSAROKA RANGE

Eagle Peak 11,358' (highest point in the park)

SHOSHONE NATIONAL FOREST

CONTINENTAL DIVIDE

BRIDGER-TETON NATIONAL FOREST

South Entrance

Flagg Ranch Information Station

GRAND TETON NATIONAL PARK

BRIDGER-TETON NATIONAL FOREST

South Entrance to Jackson, 64 miles

N

10 MILES

Paul Woodward, © 2006 The Countryman Press

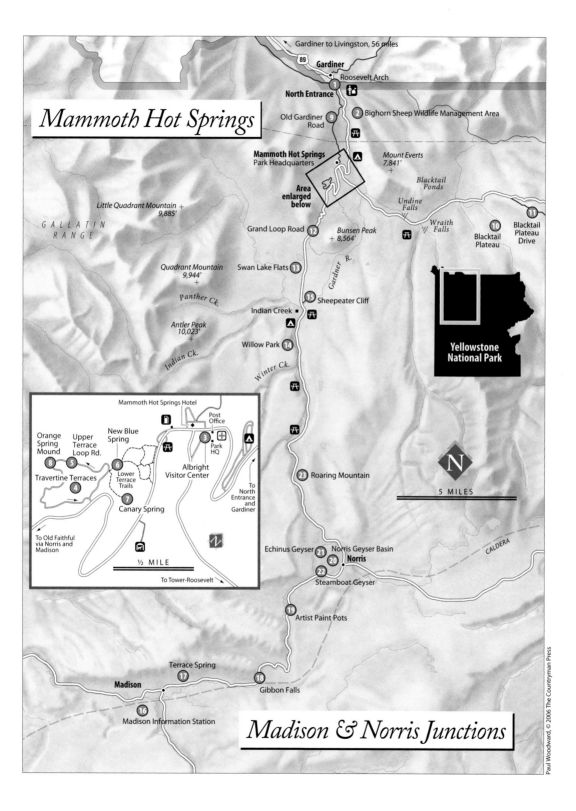

Mammoth Hot Springs

Gardiner to Livingston, 56 miles

89 **Gardiner**

Roosevelt Arch

North Entrance 1

Old Gardiner Road 9

2 Bighorn Sheep Wildlife Management Area

Mammoth Hot Springs
Park Headquarters

Mount Everts 7,841'

Area enlarged below

Blacktail Ponds

Undine Falls

Little Quadrant Mountain + 9,885'

GALLATIN RANGE

Grand Loop Road 12

Bunsen Peak + 8,564'

Wraith Falls

Blacktail Plateau 10

11 Blacktail Plateau Drive

Quadrant Mountain 9,944' +

Swan Lake Flats 13

Gardiner R.

Panther Ck.

15 Sheepeater Cliff

Indian Creek

Antler Peak 10,023' +

Willow Park 14

Indian Ck.

Winter Ck.

Yellowstone National Park

Mammoth Hot Springs Hotel

Post Office

Orange Spring Mound

Upper Terrace Loop Rd.

New Blue Spring

8 5 6

Travertine Terraces

4

Lower Terrace Trails

7

Canary Spring

3 Park HQ

Albright Visitor Center

To North Entrance and Gardiner

To Old Faithful via Norris and Madison

½ MILE

To Tower-Roosevelt

23 Roaring Mountain

N

5 MILES

CALDERA

Echinus Geyser 21

Norris Geyser Basin

20 **Norris**

22

Steamboat Geyser

19

Artist Paint Pots

Terrace Spring 17

Madison

18

Gibbon Falls

16

Madison Information Station

Madison & Norris Junctions

Paul Woodward, © 2006 The Countryman Press

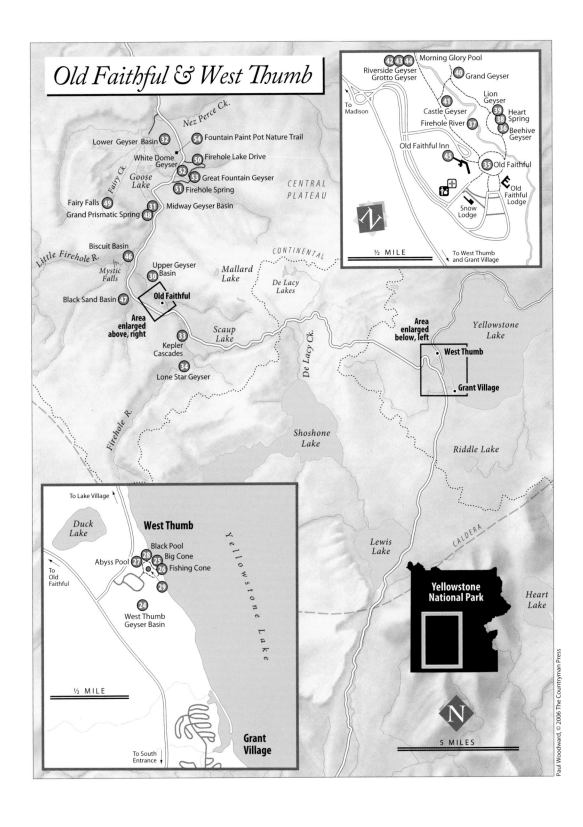

Old Faithful & West Thumb

Lower Geyser Basin **32**
Fountain Paint Pot Nature Trail **54**
White Dome Geyser
Firehole Lake Drive **50**
52
53 Great Fountain Geyser
Firehole Spring **51**
Goose Lake
Fairy Ck.

CENTRAL PLATEAU

Fairy Falls **49**
31
Grand Prismatic Spring **48**
Midway Geyser Basin

Biscuit Basin
Little Firehole R.
46
Mystic Falls
Upper Geyser Basin **30**

CONTINENTAL

Mallard Lake
De Lacy Lakes

Black Sand Basin **47**
Old Faithful

Area enlarged above, right

Scaup Lake

33
Kepler Cascades
34
Lone Star Geyser

Firehole R.

De Lacy Ck.

Shoshone Lake

Yellowstone Lake

Area enlarged below, left

West Thumb

Grant Village

Riddle Lake

Inset (top right)

Morning Glory Pool
Riverside Geyser **42 43 44**
Grotto Geyser
40 Grand Geyser
To Madison
Lion Geyser
Castle Geyser **41**
39
38 Heart Spring
Firehole River **37**
36 Beehive Geyser
Old Faithful Inn
45
35 Old Faithful
Old Faithful Lodge
Snow Lodge
½ MILE
To West Thumb and Grant Village

Inset (bottom left)

To Lake Village
Duck Lake
West Thumb
Black Pool
28 Big Cone
Abyss Pool **27** **25**
26 Fishing Cone
To Old Faithful
29
24
West Thumb Geyser Basin
Yellowstone Lake
½ MILE
Grant Village
To South Entrance

Lewis Lake

CALDERA

Yellowstone National Park

Heart Lake

N
5 MILES

Paul Woodward, © 2006 The Countryman Press

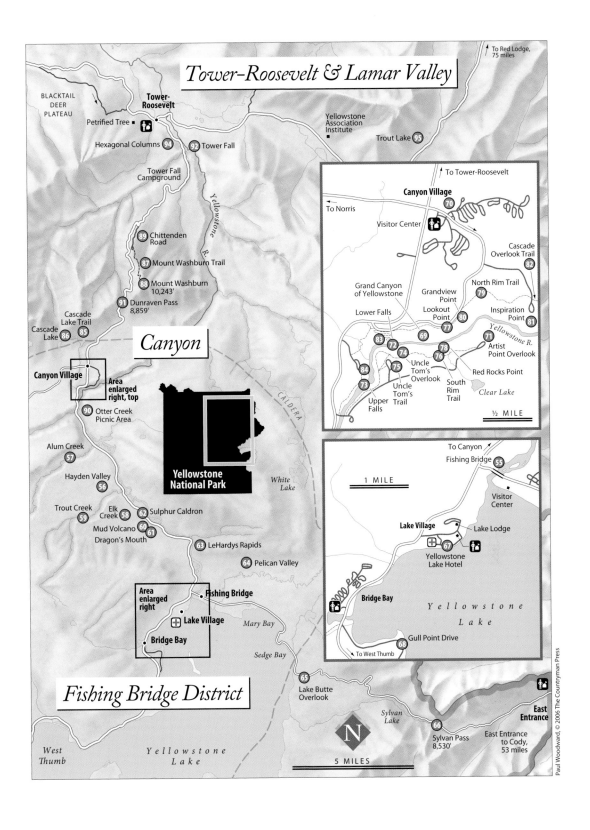

Tower-Roosevelt & Lamar Valley

To Red Lodge, 75 miles

BLACKTAIL DEER PLATEAU

Tower-Roosevelt

Petrified Tree

Yellowstone Association Institute

Hexagonal Columns (94) (92) Tower Fall

Trout Lake (95)

Tower Fall Campground

Yellowstone R.

(89) Chittenden Road

(87) Mount Washburn Trail

(88) Mount Washburn 10,243'

(91) Dunraven Pass 8,859'

Cascade Lake Trail
Cascade Lake (86) (85)

Canyon

Canyon Village

Area enlarged right, top

(90) Otter Creek Picnic Area

Alum Creek
(57)

Hayden Valley
(56)

Trout Creek
(59) Elk Creek (58) (62) Sulphur Caldron

Mud Volcano (60)
Dragon's Mouth (61)

(53) LeHardys Rapids

(64) Pelican Valley

CALDERA

White Lake

Yellowstone National Park

Area enlarged right
Fishing Bridge
Lake Village
Bridge Bay

Mary Bay

Sedge Bay

Fishing Bridge District

(65) Lake Butte Overlook

West Thumb

Yellowstone Lake

Sylvan Lake

5 MILES

N

To Tower-Roosevelt

Canyon Village

To Norris

Visitor Center

(70)

Cascade Overlook Trail (32)

Grand Canyon of Yellowstone
Grandview Point

North Rim Trail (79)

Lower Falls
Lookout Point
(80) (77)

Inspiration Point (81)

Yellowstone R.

Artist Point Overlook (71)

(83) (72)
(69)
(74)
(78)
(76)

Red Rocks Point

(84)
(75)

Uncle Tom's Overlook

South Rim Trail

(73)

Upper Falls

Uncle Tom's Trail

Clear Lake

½ MILE

To Canyon

Fishing Bridge (55)

1 MILE

Visitor Center

Lake Village Lake Lodge

(67)

Yellowstone Lake Hotel

Bridge Bay

Yellowstone Lake

Gull Point Drive (68)

To West Thumb

Sylvan Pass 8,530' (66)

East Entrance

East Entrance to Cody, 53 miles

Paul Woodward, © 2006 The Countryman Press

these form the major headings of a compass: the North Entrance from Gardiner, Montana; the West Entrance from West Yellowstone, Montana; the South Entrance from Jackson, Wyoming; and the East Entrance from Cody, Wyoming. The fifth entry, the Northeast Entrance, passes through Cooke City and Silver Gate, Wyoming, before leading into the remote northeast corner of the park.

Each passage into the park is unique and offers its own panoply of charms. Entering from the north, you'll pass under the historic Roosevelt Arch, dedicated in 1903 by President Theodore Roosevelt and rededicated on its 100th anniversary by his great grandson, Theodore Roosevelt IV, during the very summer that I was on assignment in the park. If you're arriving from the east, you may want to take in the **Buffalo Bill Museum** in Cody, Wyoming. **Grand Teton National Park** abuts Yellowstone at the south gate. Look for **moose** in the wetlands along the Lewis River just inside the park if you arrive in Yellowstone from this direction. From West Yellowstone, the road into the park follows the Madison River past meadows where you're very likely to spot your first Yellowstone elk. Along this route you'll also see striking examples of burned forest from the 1988 forest fires. Yet emerging through the duff and lingering patches of snow, note the vibrant green of new lodgepole pines under the charred skeletons of their parents.

The Northeast Entrance is my favorite. Just southwest of Red Lodge, Montana, the **Beartooth Highway** (US 212) soars to 10,000 feet above sea level as it climbs the Beartooth Plateau. After winding through vertiginous declivities and precipitous switchbacks, this amazing road emerges above the tree line, typically the exclusive domain of intrepid hikers and climbers. For roughly 15 miles, the Beartooth Highway skirts vibrant alpine meadows, shimmering glacial lakes, and small perennial gla-

ciers that cling to the shaded draws and ledges before it descends into Cook City, Montana, just outside the Northeast Entrance to Yellowstone National Park. The Beartooth Highway is one of America's top scenic highways, but if you're the one driving, be sure to use the frequent pullouts to take in its breathtaking views.

In planning your photographic tour of the park, it helps to consider Yellowstone's main attractions:

- Geothermal features (hot springs, geysers, mudpots, and fumaroles)
- Grand Canyon of Yellowstone (though the canyon qualifies as a landscape, or scenic feature, it is so remarkable that it warrants separate consideration)
- Scenery (Yellowstone Lake, the mountains, waterfalls, and wildflowers)
- Mammoth Hot Springs (a distinctive geothermal feature)
- Wildlife (Hayden and Lamar valleys)

A thorough portfolio would necessarily include some images of each of these exceptional park features.

As you might imagine, the park's major attractions are not distributed evenly throughout the park but are concentrated in particular locations. Fortunately, the villages were conveniently established with the park's outstanding attributes in mind. The towering alabaster formations of the world-famous limestone terraces greet visitors in very visible and dramatic fashion at Mammoth Hot Springs, just inside the north entrance. Meanwhile, Old Faithful village is located among the park's—indeed, the world's—most extensive geyser basins. All four of the aforementioned geothermal features, including Old Faithful geyser—located right outside the Old Faithful Visitors Center—are sprinkled along a short 7-mile stretch of the Grand Loop Road near the village. Canyon village is perched within walking distance of the north rim of the fabulous Upper and Lower Falls of the Yellowstone River. Canyon also serves as the southern gateway to Mount Washburn, whose slopes blush with Indian paintbrush in early summer and from whose summit you can photograph some of the grandest overviews of the park. On the north side of Mount Washburn, the Grand Loop Road descends steeply down toward Tower-Roosevelt, the last outpost one encounters before entering the Lamar Valley, a singular stretch of wilderness that meanders between rugged outcrops, buttes, forest, and rolling plains in plain sight of bison, pronghorn, bears, wolves, and the silver braids of the Lamar River. Lake and Grant villages are both located on the shores of Yellowstone Lake. At Fishing Bridge you can end your day on the wooden porch of the historic Lake Hotel and await the finale: the full moon rising from behind the snow-capped peaks of the majestic Absaroka Range on the far side of Yellowstone Lake as chamber music or the clarion notes of a grand piano drift out across the icy water. Or you can opt for the more rustic accommodations at Grant Village.

Unlike the scenery, wildlife is not stationary, so one cannot as easily locate a visitors center near a herd of bison or provide a map to the elusive bighorn sheep. Still, there are areas of Yellowstone that are outstanding for seeing the park's famous animals. The fertile soils and abundance of water, not to mention the lack of trees, make the moist draws and the river valleys especially good places to look for wildlife. Hayden Valley, which is just north of Fishing Bridge and the Lamar Valley, east of Tower-Roosevelt, are particularly prime locales.

I should note that this guide assumes that you are a typical summer visitor to Yellowstone. Therefore, while you can certainly use this handbook as a guide to the major features of the park year-round, the times of year and day that I've indicated for certain locations, an-

gle of the sun, distribution of wildlife, and so on will be most accurate between the end of May and the beginning of September. In the event that you are still in the planning stages of a trip to Yellowstone and have not committed yourself to a certain time of year, let me briefly offer some advice as to what Yellowstone has to offer in the different seasons.

In winter, subzero temperatures turn Yellowstone National Park into a surrealistic landscape. Clouds of steam envelop entire geyser basins, where boiling water meets the frigid air. Erupting geysers resemble thermonuclear explosions as the superheated water forms immense, brilliant white columns that billow over herds of bison and elk huddled in the relative warmth of the basins, their coats hoary with frost. The light can be ethereal, creamy, dazzling, crystalline . . . phenomenal. If you can tolerate severe cold, a great deal of original work awaits you in Yellowstone in winter. Wildlife (except hibernating bears) that retreated to secluded, higher elevations during the warm months have now gathered in the valleys. Moreover, the animals are more concerned about keeping warm and finding food than avoiding you and your camera. This is an especially good time to photograph the gray wolf. The road from the Northeast Entrance through the Lamar Valley, where wolves are most frequently encountered, is accessible by automobile all the way to Mammoth Hot Springs, while access to the remainder of the park is by snow coach, snowmobile, snowshoes, and cross-country skis.

Mid-May through mid-June is an excellent time to visit Yellowstone. Daytime temperatures are cool to mild, and thus wildlife—including bighorn sheep and grizzlies—still frequent the lowlands and are easy to spot from the Grand Loop Road throughout the day. The mountains remain extensively snowcapped, and lingering patches of snow in the shaded

East fire

valleys lend an additional flair to the landscape. Newborn bison calves are nursing. Moreover, you can avoid the peak summer rush of visitors and frequently find yourself alone—photographing a coyote traversing a sparkling snow-field or a bighorn ram posing on a ledge—and feeling almost as though you had the park all to yourself.

July and August is when most people visit Yellowstone. The weather in July is perfect: cool, clear mornings and dry, comfortable sunny days with puffy white clouds nearly without fail. August, however, brings storms and lightening and, depending on your point of view, another exciting photographic subject: forest fires. August is also when the bison are

14 Photographing Yellowstone National Park

filled by early morning.) Get out of bed early, and remain in the field until the last bit of light in the evening to see the wildlife that come out into the open meadows at dawn and dusk but retreat into the cooler woods during the middle of the day.

Fall is another very good time to be in Yellowstone. The park is painted in autumn colors, and in September the elk go into rut. Their magnificent antlers have shed their "velvet"—the fuzzy skin that actually deposits the bone of the growing antlers—revealing the famed rack. The chances that you'll witness and photograph a pair of bulls in combat with one another in September through early October are exceptional. Again, keep your distance as these animals are extremely confrontational this time of year and not at all discriminating about with whom they pick a fight.

Finally, I recommend that you spend a minimum of four to five days in Yellowstone. A full week would be ideal. This would allow you to revisit areas several times in the not-too-uncommon event that your first visit was not as fruitful as you had hoped—say, the wolves didn't come out in the Lamar Valley on the particular evening you had scheduled to be in that district of the park, or it was cloudy the morning you went to photograph the rainbow on the Lower Falls. A week would enable you to thoroughly photograph and enjoy the major features of Yellowstone National Park at a relaxing pace.

rutting and the only time you can get photos of battling bulls! If you're visiting during these months, be sure to give yourself a bit more time to get from one part of the park to another. Plan ahead. You'll need to make lodging or campground reservations well in advance. (Some campgrounds do offer campsites on a first-come, first-serve basis, though they tend to be

Elk in Yellowstone National Park

Yellowstone National Park is divided into separate districts—Norris and Madison, Mammoth, Tower-Roosevelt, Canyon, Old Faithful, and Fishing Bridge—and villages that offer tidy clusters of facilities, including lodging, food services, camping, a general store, a service station, a ranger station, and a National Park Service information center. A 142-mile paved road, called the Grand Loop Road (12), cuts a figure eight through the heart of the park and connects all the villages. Unless you're camping in the backcountry or lodging outside the park, you will be staying in or near one of these villages. These districts, therefore, provide a convenient framework for planning your itinerary within the park as well for organizing this guide.

After reading the introduction and the photographic strategy and equipment sections, you can read about the photographable opportunities in and near each of the districts of Yellowstone in the order in which you visit them. Thus, this book will serve as a personal guide as you move through the park from village to village, no matter where on the loop road you wish to begin.

Gustav W. Verderber

Sunrise on Yellowstone Lake

Within the district chapters, major attractions, subjects, and points of interest are printed in boldface. The appendix contains several suggested daily itineraries to help you make the most of your precious time in Yellowstone, along with photographic data for all the photos included in this guide, for photo enthusiasts who want to know what equipment, film, and camera settings were used for each.

How I Photograph Yellowstone National Park

Knowing where to look for what subjects is only part of the photographic game. It's also important to know *when* to look—and when *not* to look. At times the savvy photographer will forgo a favorite subject and pursue some other photographic quarry that, owing to the prevailing weather, time of day, and season, might be more conducive to producing outstanding images. Additionally, various subjects demand a variety of photographic techniques and equipment. Clearly a different strategy is required to photograph wildlife—especially animals that, when provoked, could harm or even kill you—than would be suitable for wildflowers or scenics.

When Kodak invited me to be the Kodak Ambassador in Yellowstone in 2003, I participated in the annual training that all seasonal rangers undergo before receiving their badges and uniforms and taking up their posts at the visitor centers and on the trails throughout the park. Following that orientation, I had one week prior to beginning my assignment for Kodak to explore the park on my own. I had never before been to Yellowstone, yet by following a system, at the end of that glorious week, I had produced a publishable portfolio that included bighorn sheep, hot springs, geysers (including Old Faithful), the Lower Falls of the Grand Canyon of Yellowstone, Yellowstone Lake, coyotes, grizzly bears, bison, and osprey. I was able to photograph all of these subjects not because I am a professional nature photographer, but because I followed some simple guidelines that helped me increase the odds of being in the right place at the right time.

I will outline the overall photographic strategy I used to create all the images that illustrate this book during my first visit to Yellowstone National Park.

Honestly, you do not need a Ph.D. to take a great photograph. Good thing—because I don't have one. All it takes is some common sense, a good deal of diligence, the right light, and a dash of luck. We are in charge of the first two, the third is merely a matter of timing, and that last ingredient—well, you know what someone once said about luck: It's nothing more than preparation meeting opportunity.

Here's what I did.

First, I read everything I had been given by the ranger at the gate when I initially entered the park. I studied the park map and familiarized myself with the park rules. Next, I spent some time in one of the visitors centers gathering additional information, browsing in the bookstore, and talking with the interpretive rangers. We pored over the park map, and they provided valuable insights about the distribution of wildlife within the park. Animals migrate between varying habitats throughout the year as they follow available forage and prey, avoid excessive heat, cold, and deep snow. Being primarily familiar with species east of the Mississippi, I was not attuned to the movements of grizzly bears, pronghorn, bighorn sheep, and bison. Without the rangers' advice, I would have wasted a great deal of precious time looking for wildlife in all the wrong places. Following my chat with the rangers, I bought a few field guides to add to my library, and I also picked up a collection of trail guides to each of the park's major areas (Old Faithful, Mammoth, and Canyon, for example). These guides pinpoint all the significant attractions within the separate districts and include a detailed map, brief descriptions of the attractions and hiking trails, distances, and locations of facilities. These trail guides are not part of the

Gustav W. Verderber

Fishing Cone at sunrise

package you receive when you enter the park, but they can be purchased at any of the visitors centers for a small donation. They are truly indispensable mini-handbooks to the park.

By the end of my first day in Yellowstone, I was ready to begin plotting my strategy for photographing the park, and I made a preliminary list of the locations I wanted to visit and in what order. Each night I set my travel alarm and got up early every morning—and I mean *real* early: 4:30 AM—so that I could be in the field by sunrise, which in June occurs around 5:30. I know. You're on vacation. Yet to a large degree, this is essentially what separates pros from amateurs: They do what they must to be wherever they need to be, whenever they need to be there, to get the image. Similarly, if you truly wish to come away with some amazing photographs that you can proudly display on your living room wall, then I strongly encourage you to get out of bed or your sleeping bag at or before the crack of dawn.

I worked the major wildlife areas first thing in the morning, principally the Hayden and Lamar valleys, depending on in which part of the park I had spent the night. The air is cool at this time of the day, even in midsummer, and animals are out and about, clearly visible in these vast open areas. What's more, wildlife will be radiant in the early-morning sunlight; their faces are beautifully lit, and their eyes sparkle. In the middle of the day, the harsh overhead sun creates too much contrast between the shaded sides of large animals—especially bison, elk, and grizzlies—and the bright, horizontal surfaces of the surrounding landscape. Faces are dark, and eyes appear dull and lifeless in photographs. On the other hand, smaller animals, like ground squirrels and marmots, which present a flatter perspective toward the sky, get wonderful light on their faces and in their eyes even at high noon, particularly if they are facing south.

By 9:00 AM animals seek shade and retreat to the woods, where they bed down and remain out of sight until the cool air returns in the evening. It's fruitless to go looking for wildlife between 9:00 AM and 6:00 PM during the summer.

When the wildlife weren't cooperating, I concentrated on landscapes, creating compositions with the Yellowstone or Lamar rivers running like gold and silver ribbons through my viewfinder; on occasion, I headed for the West Thumb Geyser Basin, where I knew I could line up the sunrise with the lake and a geyser or a hot spring in the foreground. As you peruse the individual sections of this book, you'll find that I mention other morning locations. In any event, dawn is not to be squandered in Yellowstone.

In the vicinity of the Upper and Lower Falls (so named because of their respective relative positions upstream and downstream from one another), in the Grand Canyon of the Yellowstone, the Yellowstone River runs generally west to east. Thus both falls receive morning light. This is where you'll want to head following your early-morning wildlife excursions.

On one morning, wrap up your dawn wildlife safari a bit early and arrive at the canyon area around 7:00 AM. It's at this time that the sun clears the canyon's north rim and brilliantly illuminates the Lower Falls. The rich light appears to turn the cliffs on either side of the plunging river to bronze, saturating the vivid ochre stains produced by oxidizing iron compounds in the volcanic rhyolite that forms the canyon walls. One of my favorite views of the Lower Falls is from Artist Point on the south rim. Yet sunrise from Artist Point is only a prelude to the canyon's feature presentation.

Around the time the animals begin to aban-don the valleys for the forests, I typically headed for the canyon area to arrive at one of the south or north rim overlooks between 8:00 and 8:30 AM. From 8:00 to 10:00 AM, the sun rounds the southeast arc of its path over the canyon and forms just the right angle with respect to the river to paint resplendent rainbows on both the Upper and Lower Falls. These views of the falls, particularly of Lower Falls, when the rainbow appears in the mist at the bottom of the cascade, are among the most remarkable natural spectacles I have witnessed anywhere on Earth. This show is not to be missed! (See my detailed description of the canyon area in Chapter 5 for precise times to view the rainbows from the different lookouts.)

Generally, and for reasons I identified above, the best nature photos are taken early and late in the day, when the sun is low or even below the horizon, and the light is subdued and heavily influenced by the longer wavelengths—that is, the red end of the spectrum. Photographers call it "warm" light. Still, there are exceptions, and Yellowstone is replete with subjects that look their best in bright sunlight.

During the middle of the day, from 10:00 AM to 4:00 PM, I would casually wander around the various geyser basins, photographing the geothermal features. Indeed, the only time one can capture the surreal colors of the hot springs, the dazzling cobalt water and the vibrant halos of the bacterial mats, is at high noon on a clear, sunny day, when the sun is as close to a 90-degree angle relative to the surface of the pool as is possible at 45-degree north latitude—the latitude of Yellowstone. (During the summer, Wyoming is on daylight savings time, so solar noon occurs at 1:00 PM.) Earlier in the morning or later in the afternoon, the strong index of refraction of water bends the light away from the bottom of the pool—where all the color is—and the hot springs are not nearly as resplendent. Mudpots (boiling mud) also lend themselves to midday photography, especially if you want sufficient light to freeze that bubble of mud as it bursts.

The best time to photograph a geyser—no surprise—is when it's erupting. For that reason, I would always drop into the nearest visitors center to check that day's geyser schedule and try to coordinate my itinerary with an impending eruption. Remember that any visitors center anywhere in Yellowstone will have the day's schedule of eruptions for all the predictable geysers in the park, regardless of their location. (Yellowstone has over 300 geysers, but only a handful of the major ones, most of them in the Upper Geyser Basin, are predicted.)

Fumaroles, on the other hand, spew forth steam continuously. I photographed these as I encountered them.

Note that all the photography I have described so far assumes that the weather is clear and sunny. Wildlife eyes don't gleam as brightly, rainbows don't form, and hot springs don't dazzle on overcast days. Erupting geysers barely show up against a cloudy sky. Thus, on overcast days—which are rare from May through July—I often headed for Mammoth Hot Springs. The limestone formations there resemble alabaster; many are too bright to stand direct sunlight. I enjoyed finding compositions among the terraces whenever the light was too dull to photograph wildlife, the geyser basins, or the canyon area.

As the day waned, I typically returned to the valleys to look for wildlife. My favorite after-dinner drive was along the East Entrance road from Fishing Bridge to Sylvan Pass. The north side of the road, notably at Mary Bay and Sedge Bay, is drenched in golden late-afternoon light. Look for yellow-bellied marmots lounging on the lichen-covered rocks. Most of all, watch for grizzly bears. From May through July, this stretch is very good for photographing grizzlies—from the safety of your vehicle—

as they graze on the prolific sulfur flowers in the meadows and alongside the road. The road is hemmed in by Yellowstone Lake toward the south and a low ridge that parallels the north side of the road for several miles. Thus, the lake and the ridge form a narrow corridor so that if a bear is within view, it will likely be grazing only a few yards from the road—and your car. On numerous occasions I had grizzlies complacently feeding on the shoulder of the road just 15 feet from my lens! Of course, it is imperative that you remain in your vehicle when a grizzly is this close. In fact, since the bears are accustomed to cars, the best photographic strategy is simply to pull off the road ahead of the bruin and then photograph it as it grazes past your car window.

True artists know when to stick to the basic guidelines that initially helped us learn how to take a simple photograph and when a skillful violation of the rules may result in an exceptional image. Until you become adept at bending let alone breaking those rules—successfully—always take the standard (i.e., front lit) photograph first to assure that you have some good photos "in the can." Then if you have the chance, experiment and work the subject: Shoot vertical as well as horizontal composi-

Gustav W. Verderber

Grizzly bear

tions (but always make sure that the animal is facing into rather than out of the photograph), alter the background and lighting by shifting your position, view the subject from a variety of angles, and if the subject is moving, use different shutter speeds. Freeze the motion of an animal's head and torso, but allow the legs—which are moving faster than the rest of the body—to appear slightly blurred. (Bracketing around 1/60th of a second works best.) This suggests motion and lends tension and drama to a photograph. As they do in the movies, tension and drama grab people's attention and make for extremely compelling photographs. In other words, people will want to see your work!

Only by experimenting and evaluating your results will you become sufficiently familiar with your equipment and the subjects you enjoy photographing most to feel confident about breaking the rules again in the future. Of course, this learning process requires that you take notes so that you can recall which techniques were successful and which were not. After 20 years of photographing nature, I still keep field notes, diligently recording in a small notebook I keep in my camera bag my exposure (F-stop and shutter speed), type of film or digital ISO and shooting mode, how I metered the light, whether I used a strobe or filters, the strobe settings and flash-subject distance, location, date, and pertinent natural history information. Otherwise, each time I were to venture into the field with my camera, I would have only the fundamental rules at my disposal, and though I might produce some fine photographs, my abilities would never improve beyond some mediocre level because I wouldn't have learned to work outside those basic parameters. Moreover, I would have cheated myself out of having genuinely explored the extent of my creative potential.

The plan I've outlined here enabled me to be in the most productive parts of the park at the most promising times of the day and thereby maximize my photographic opportunities from sunrise to sunset. By following this overall itinerary and incorporating appropriate substitutions when you feel you have sufficient photographs of a particular subject—for example, going to West Thumb to photograph the sunrise instead of the canyon or heading to Gibbon Meadows for elk rather than pursuing bison in Hayden Valley—you will systematically work all the major areas of the park and give yourself as good a chance as any professional photographer of bringing home a fabulously diverse portfolio of Yellowstone National Park.

Equipment

The assortment of photo gear you bring into the field depends on whether you pursue photography as a hobby or a profession as well as on your personal style, financial resources, favorite subject(s), and what's practical in a given situation. Thus it would be presumptuous of me to prescribe precisely what cameras, lenses, films, filters, and so on would work best for every photographer in Yellowstone. That said, however, some equipment is absolutely necessary for making excellent rather than mediocre images, equipment that will make you more efficient and reduce aggravation in the field, and even some gear that may save your life. Yellowstone is not a benign location; every year visitors get hurt attempting to get wonderful photos of the park—in particular, of its temperamental wildlife. Beyond being convenient, being properly equipped in Yellowstone will also help keep you out of harm's way.

You must ask yourself two fundamental questions whenever you invest in photographic equipment:

1) What camera(s), lenses, and accessories will do the job most efficiently?

2) What do I intend to do with my photographs after I've created them?

The subjects you intend to photograph (say, portraits, wildlife, landscapes, sports), cost, and practicality (ease of use under the circumstances) are among the factors that will help you answer the first question. The second question pertains to your aspirations as a photographer—whether you ultimately want to turn professional, enter your top photos in a camera-club contest, post them on a Web site, produce a slide show for your school or local nature center, or frame a few good prints for your living room wall. A teacher interested in illustrating a lecture with projected images taken on vacation does not need the same outfit as does a professional who's selling photos to discriminating editors at top national and international magazines or stock agencies.

With this in mind, the equipment listed below is what any serious photographer would pack in a camera bag on a trip to Yellowstone National Park.

Digital or 35mm single-lens-reflex (SLR) camera body with interchangeable lenses

An SLR camera body is any body with a viewfinder that allows you to look directly through the lens and shows you *exactly* what the lens sees. A rangefinder camera, on the other hand, has a separate window—usually positioned in the upper-left corner of the body—that does not allow you to look directly through the lens. Consequently, there will be a noticeable difference (that increases as your distance to the subject decreases) between what you see and the actual image you make with a rangefinder camera. Simply put, serious nature photographers do not use rangefinder cameras.

Fortunately, the quality of digital technology has caught up with film. The major camera manufacturers are producing digital cameras whose resolution (image sharpness) rivals their 35mm counterparts, and many professional photographers have forsaken their film cameras for digital models. By definition, the camera you already own is a good camera. However, if you are serious about photography and have not yet invested in a photographic system, I would encourage you to choose a digital SLR camera. Though film will not become obsolete any time soon, digital photography offers possibilities to share and present your images quickly and easily without having to wait for the developed film to come back from the lab. Best of all, digital cameras let you immediately know if you captured the photograph you were hoping for and allow you to make appropriate adjustments and correct mistakes while your subject is still in front of your camera. That advantage by itself merits the switch to digital technology.

Some features to look for on a camera body, digital or film, include fully manual as well as automatic exposure modes (to be a proficient photographer, you must be in full control of exposure rather than leave your aperture and shutter speed settings entirely up to the camera), a depth-of-field preview button for determining focus on landscapes and close-ups, a mirror lock-up option for sharper photos, autofocus capability to make wildlife photography easier, and the ability to use a wide range of lenses on the body.

Focal lengths ranging from a minimum of 50 to 200mm; ideally, 24 to 300mm

If you hope to photograph everything Yellowstone has to offer, from sweeping landscapes to the wildlife, you'll need a lens or lenses to cover this range of focal lengths. Indeed, there are zoom lenses that can focus from 28 to 200mm or even from 80 to 400mm. Bear in mind, how-

Bison grazing

ever, that the greater the range of focal lengths a zoom lens includes, the more you compromise the resolution.

By browsing through the Photographic Data chart on page 88, you will quickly get an overview of the equipment I used to photograph the park. Notice that I frequently used my 50mm (also known as a "normal" lens since subjects viewed through this focal length appear normal in size and distance) to photograph most of the landscapes and geysers and herds of wildlife in Yellowstone. Now and again I used a 200mm telephoto lens (any focal length longer than 50mm is referred to as "telephoto") to pull in a distant landscape feature, and wide-angle (focal lengths less than 50mm) shots are rare.

Photographing animals is another matter. A 200mm telephoto lens is the minimum focal length for photographing the wildlife in Yellowstone at a safe distance. At this magnification you will not have to explain that the dark spec in the image is a bison, a bear, or a moose; the animals will at least be recognizable for what they are, though they will not nearly fill the viewfinder. As a matter of fact, it's a good idea to include the scenery around the subject simply to demonstrate that the animal was indeed photographed in Yellowstone. Otherwise people might think that you photographed that bison or bear at the zoo. I typically photographed the wildlife with focal lengths up to 600mm, but you must remember that I sell my photographs to extremely discriminating editors. If I can't sell my photos, I don't eat.

You must decide for yourself how demanding a photographer you want to be. Before you leave for Yellowstone, become familiar with the

Gustav W. Verderber

magnification of various focal lengths at your local camera shop and match the right equipment with your personal goals.

Very often you'll be using your telephoto lens to photograph moving wildlife. Sometimes you won't have time even to mount your camera on a tripod. While I don't find it necessary for my short focal length lenses to be equipped with auto-focus and image-stabilization technology (lenses with built-in gyros that dampen movement of the camera and lens), auto-focus, image-stabilized telephoto lenses do make staying focused on distant moving targets and hand-held photography *much* easier. Indeed, I could not produce high-quality photographs of wildlife as consistently without the auto-focus and image-stabilization technology incorporated into many contemporary lenses. So if wildlife is your thing, and you can justify—and afford—the added expense, I would encourage you to consider auto-focus and image-stabilizing technology when assembling your photographic outfit.

You should know that frame-filling images of elusive and dangerous wildlife are typically taken with 600mm or longer telephoto lenses—or, quite frankly, the subjects are not wild animals. Many photographers use exotic game ranches to photograph "wildlife" at close range. Do not incur undo risks to yourself or the truly wild inhabitants of Yellowstone by trying to do the impossible—that is, emulating the covers of the portfolio books you see in the visitor center bookstores with inappropriate equipment.

Tripod, cable release, bean bag

Good technique is as valuable but much less expensive than longer lenses and space-age technology. Simple practices such as holding your breath when you squeeze the shutter button, bracing yourself against a tree, or using a tripod whenever possible will significantly improve the quality of your photography. Your images will always be sharper if you take a moment to mount your camera on a tripod before tripping the shutter. Nobody, not even a neurosurgeon, can hold a camera as rock steady as a tripod. Additionally, a tripod enables you to spend more time thinking about and fine tuning the composition, and it reduces strain by holding the camera for you while you're waiting for an animal to turn its head toward you.

When I'm photographing stationary subjects, I use a cable release to avoid jarring the camera as I push the shutter button. If the situation allows, I also eliminate the vibration produced by the mirror inside the camera as it swings out of the way of the shutter by using my mirror lock-up option once I'm satisfied with the composition. Yet when I'm photographing wildlife, I remove the cable release, preferring instead to keep my hand on the camera and my eye behind the viewfinder with my finger on the shutter button so that I can focus, shoot, and maintain the animal—which is typically moving—exactly where I want it in my composition.

Understandably, there will be many occasions in Yellowstone when there will be no time or it will not be safe for you to get out of your car and set up a tripod, as in the case described above of the grizzlies grazing by the side of the East Entrance road. Such "drive-by shootings" are numerous in Yellowstone, and you have to be ready for them. In these instances you will have to take your photographs from your vehicle. Therefore, *always*, *always* keep your camera loaded, cocked, and handy when you're driving around the park.

The handiest tool I have for shooting out of the window of my truck is also one of the cheapest: a small pillowcase stuffed with dried beans. With the driver window rolled down, this homemade "bean bag" rests securely on the window frame. I can nestle even my longest telephoto lenses snugly on the pillow and easily move the camera horizontally and vertically to get perfectly sharp photos of the wildlife.

Polarizing and skylight filters

I do not use filters extensively to enhance my images or to create special effects.

Nature does that for me. Instead, I make it my job to be there for those ephemeral moments when the light is rare and the moment is genuinely unique. Nevertheless, there are times when a filter is warranted.

A polarizing filter eliminates or reduces *reflected* light. Such a filter achieves the same effect that a pair of polarizing sunglasses has on the glare on the windshield of a car: It enables you to see through the glare. Thus I used a polarizing filter extensively to photograph the hot springs throughout Yellowstone. The filter eliminated the surface reflections, thereby saturating the striking colors of the thermal bacteria that ring the substrate around the shallow edges of the pool as well as the deep, sapphire center. A polarizer also creates a stark contrast between white clouds—or, for that matter, the white water of an erupting geyser—and blue sky. Keep in mind, however, that at 8,000 feet above sea level in Yellowstone, the sky is already extremely blue. Thus a polarizing filter could turn the sky an unnatural navy blue and give your landscapes a fake appearance. But just attach the polarizer to your lens to see the effect it will have on your exposure, and then decide whether you want to use it or not.

Whenever I was strolling around a geyser basin, I was careful to put either a polarizing filter or a skylight filter on my lenses. A skylight filter reduces atmospheric haze and color casts caused by UV light, of which the latter is more of a problem in Yellowstone due, again, to its high altitude. Either of these filters serves another important function: They prevent your lenses from being damaged by the sulfuric acid in the geyser spray. Obviously the first precau-

tion is to avoid standing downwind of erupting geysers; the caustic spray will immediately dissolve the coatings right off your expensive lenses and ruin them. For good. Second, you can safeguard your lenses simply by covering them with a filter. If the wind shifts, and you and your camera are accidentally sprayed by an erupting geyser, it's far less painful to replace a $20 filter than a $1,500 lens.

Extension tubes or macro lens

If you are keen to get close-ups of wildflowers, insects, or the unique geology of Yellowstone, than I recommend that you pick up a kit of extension tubes. These are hollow spacers that you mount between your lens and the camera body, thereby moving the lens farther from the film or digital sensor. The greater the distance from the lens to the photographic medium, the closer you can get to your subject and still be in focus—consequently, the more you magnify the image of the subject. The beauty of extension tubes, unlike magnifying filters or diopters that you screw on the front of your lens is that they do not reduce resolution by introducing additional glass between the subject and the film or sensor. And they are quite affordable. Extension tubes typically come in a kit of three tubes, each a different length, that you can use individually or stack to achieve a wide range of close-up magnifications behind fixed-focal length or zoom lenses.

A macro lens is a lens designed to focus closer on a subject, and thereby provide increased magnification, without any additional components being added in front of or behind the lens. For example, you can buy a 50mm normal lens or a 50mm macro lens. Both lenses work virtually identically as landscape lenses, but the significantly closer minimal focusing distance of the 50mm macro is less than half that of the normal version, giving you about twice as much magnification. Alas, macro lenses are very expensive, so I suggest that you put some extension tubes behind whatever lens you already own before investing in a macro.

Film and/or memory cards

The rule of thumb for choosing film is: After you've decided whether you want color or black and white, prints or slides, choose the slowest speed (ASA rating) film that will enable you to get sharp shots under the conditions you expect to be photographing. The slower the film, the finer the grain, and the sharper the images. This is an especially important consideration if you anticipate making enlargements to hang in your home or office. At enlargements greater than 8 by 10 inches, the coarse grain of fast films (ASA 200 and up) becomes apparent and reduces the quality of the image.

Outdoors at an elevation of 8,000 feet, lack of light is not a problem in Yellowstone. I had ample light during my sojourn in the park to photograph all of my landscapes on ASA 50 film. For wildlife I used ASA 100 to make up for the light lost through long telephoto lenses (the greater the focal length, the less light that reaches the camera) and allow me to use faster shutter speeds to freeze the motion of the moving subjects.

Another consideration in picking your film is whether you anticipate holding your camera or mounting it on a tripod. Indeed, there are situations in which the use of a tripod is not an option—for example, those unanticipated drive-by shootings I mentioned earlier. Telephoto lenses don't selectively magnify only the subject you wish to photograph; they magnify everything, including the relative motion of the subject and the camera. The longer the lens, the more motion the film "sees." To freeze that motion and get a sharp shot of the subject, you necessarily need a faster shutter speed. So the longer the lens, the faster the required shutter speed. Here, the rule of thumb is that whenever a cam-

era is handheld, you should not use a shutter speed slower than the inverse of the focal length of the lens. For example, with a 50mm lens, you aren't likely to get a sharp image if you use a shutter speed slower than 1/50th of a second. With a 300mm lens, you would have to use shutter speeds of 1/300th of a second or faster to assure a sharp photo. Therefore, the light or the film speed would have to be sufficient to allow you to use those faster shutter speeds.

Camera bag and field bag

If you plan on doing any hiking in Yellowstone, you will need an efficient means of comfortably carrying your camera gear, film, water, nourishment, maps, field glasses, a jacket, and perhaps your bear repellant and field guides into the wilderness. A sturdy backpack, perhaps combined with a belly pack, to accommodate everything you need to wander away from the road even a short distance, will considerably enhance your enjoyment and safety within the park.

Whenever I encountered a photo opportunity that required leaving my truck, no matter how anxious I was to begin photographing, I *always* locked my vehicle, slipped on my backpack—which contained all of my camera gear and a windbreaker—and strapped on my belly pack with two bottles of fresh water, some trail mix, several rolls of film, a park map, a compass, notebook and pen, and bear spray. I frequently pulled over and got out of my truck to grab a shot of a group of elk or pronghorn, expecting to spend only a few moments behind the camera—and then found myself, an hour or two later, a mile or more from my truck, having exposed several rolls of film as I carefully followed the animals while they wandered farther and farther into the back country. So long as I had my backpack, belly pack, and tripod, I knew I had everything I needed to keep me safe and happily focused on the task at hand: capturing the wonders of Yellowstone.

"FOR THE BENEFIT AND
ENJOYMENT OF THE PEOPLE"
YELLOWSTONE
NATIONAL
PARK
CREATED BY
ACT OF CONGRESS
MARCH 1, 1872

Jett Hitt

Roosevelt Arch with rainbow

I. Mammoth Hot Springs

Roosevelt Arch (1)

The imposing **Roosevelt Arch, (1),** so named after its dedication by President Theodore Roosevelt in 1903, towers over the North Entrance to Yellowstone and serves as the formal gateway to the park. It is much more than merely a portico to the world's first national park—a designated World Heritage Site and Biosphere Reserve—and over 2 million acres of some of the most outstanding wilderness on Earth. It is a monument that celebrates the recognition by a democratic society of the importance of public lands set aside for all the people and belonging to all the people—indeed, the inscription on the Roosevelt Arch proclaims that Yellowstone exits FOR THE BENEFIT AND ENJOYMENT OF THE PEOPLE. It also recognizes a place where wild nature is free—of human imposition, private ownership, and exploitation—and allowed to follow its own imperative. In this park the intrinsic value of our natural environment supercedes the commodity values that we impose on the overwhelming majority of the planet's ecosystems. It is a place where we can genuinely encounter nature on its own terms.

The arch is best viewed either in the morning or afternoon, when the sun's summer ecliptic takes it slightly north of the arch and illuminates the north-facing side, the side with the inscription. Personally, I am hardly ever inclined to get into my own photographs as in, "Here I am standing in front of Old Faithful." Yet, the Roosevelt Arch by itself appears somewhat stark. Unless you're fortunate enough to frame a passing elk or bison, let alone a rainbow under the arch, I would indeed recommend that you set the self-timer on your camera and get that shot of yourself striking a pose under the gateway into our greatest homage to the American wilderness.

Bighorn Sheep Wildlife Management Area (2)

As you enter Yellowstone from the North Entrance, be sure to notice the rugged cliffs that rise steeply from the east side of the road between the Roosevelt Arch and Mammoth. These rocks are part of a **Bighorn Sheep Wildlife Management Area (2),** an area preserved and managed as critical habitat for bighorn sheep. Remember to look for individuals or groups of sheep along the cliffs whenever you leave or return to the park since the odds are very good that you might spot a ewe (female) or ram (male) precariously perched on a slim ledge or scree slope. Both rams and ewes sport horns, yet those of an adult ram curl around almost in an entire circle. Although they are adapted to such precarious, rocky en-

Gustav W. Verderber

Bighorn ram

vironments, bighorn sheep do have accidents. Just as you and I occasionally trip or slip, bighorn sheep sometimes fall off cliffs, slip on icy slopes, or are swept away in an avalanche.

Albright Visitors Center (3)

Anyone visiting Yellowstone National Park for the first time is apt to be overwhelmed by the seemingly inexhaustible photo opportunities the park has to offer. When you arrive in the park through the North Entrance, you can allay your apprehension by merely dropping into the **Albright Visitors Center (3)** and availing yourself of the insights provided by the interpretive staff and the library of guides, maps, and other references. Take a few moments to share your plans with the ranger. At a minimum, be sure to pick up a map of the park and one of each of the individual trail guides to the different park districts. These point the way to all the outstanding features within each district. Then, relax over a meal in the restaurant, study the maps and guides, and plan your adventure. Organization is the key to enjoying the park as well as to being in the right place at the right time to capture those ephemeral moments that are key to creating truly compelling photographs.

Typically, a herd of elk will be loitering on the lawns around the Albright Visitors Center and the Mammoth Hotel. Unless an especially magnificent bull elk is among them and lending himself to some tight head shots with a telephoto lens through which you can blur the background, I wouldn't bother wasting much time with these animals. It will be difficult for you to isolate your subjects from the buildings and crowds of people and get much more than a snapshot, let alone a photo that depicts a wild elk in its natural habitat. There will be, as they say, many more where these came from in more genuine surroundings.

And by the way, these elk strewn on the lawns around Mammoth like so many lawn ornaments are definitely not tame. They are truly wild animals—as dangerous, unpredictable, and as aggressive as the elk you might encounter in the backcountry. When provoked, they are as likely to charge and trample you as walk away.

The numerous burrows that pockmark the lawn directly across from the Albright Visitors Center belong to a colony of **Uinta ground squirrels**. Much like their slightly larger cousin the prairie dog, this species also prefers cleared areas, including pastures, sagebrush, and mountain meadows. Thus, wherever there are grazing animals like elk, pronghorn, or bison, you're likely to see these nervous little rodents busily chasing insects, munching on forbs and grasses, or propped like statuettes by their burrows, making sure the coast is clear of their numerous predators—notably, bears that dig them up as a snack, birds of prey, weasels, coyotes, badgers, and wolves. Owing to their familiarity with people and their size, which allows one to isolate an individual against a completely natural background, if you desire a photo of this species, take advantage of the relatively easy pickings in the picnic area in front of the visitors center, perhaps while you enjoy a sandwich.

Let's assume that you've driven or ridden a long way to get to Yellowstone and that you might be eager to stretch your legs or walk off that meal you just enjoyed while orienting yourself with the park. I have just the thing to limber you up.

Travertine Terraces (4)

Immediately upon your arrival in Mammoth, you can't help but notice the famed **Travertine Terraces (4)** rising like a mound of melted candle wax just beyond the restaurant and general store. These are limestone deposits laid down

Green algae patterns on Travertine Terrace

that feeds the hot springs at the top of the formations, temporarily restricting flow to one formation while increasing it to another. Look for the more colorful, active terraces. Much like snow, the terraces are difficult to photograph in direct sunlight. I preferred to spend time searching for compositions among the extremely bright deposits in subdued light—that is, lightly overcast, hazy-bright sunlight. However, close-ups of the abstract patterns of colors imparted to the rock by the minerals and microorganisms just off the boardwalk require bright overhead light. Thus, other than on heavily overcast days, you can always find compelling compositions among these remarkable natural sculptures. And if you're lucky, on a particularly cool morning you might catch an **elk** lounging on top of one of the terraces, cozily warming itself in the steam—a very coveted photo opportunity.

by mineral-laden water cascading from numerous hot springs that spill over the top of the mounds. Ancillary minerals, such as iron, color the white limestone in various shades of yellow, orange, and red. Additionally, various species of algae and bacteria thrive in these warm, wet settings and lend shades of green to the palette of colors that marble the facades of these enormous terraces (enormous + hot springs = Mammoth Hot Springs).

The **lower terraces** are easily viewed and photographed with normal to wide-angle and short telephoto lenses (24 to 100mm) from the boardwalk that gradually ascends the flanks of the formations and loops around, several times, to afford views of all the terraces. You will notice that some terraces are active and wet while others are dormant and dry. Frequent changes in the hydrothermal activity occasionally redirect the stream of underground water

Upper Terrace Loop Road (5), New Blue Spring (6), and Canary Spring (7)

About a mile south of the lower terrace area, look for a one-way road on the west side of the Grand Loop Road. This is the **Upper Terrace Loop Road (5)**. Follow this road for more astounding views of the travertine terraces and to observe many of the hot springs responsible for their formation. From the parking lot at the top of the Upper Terraces, you can follow a boardwalk to panoramic and close-up views of yet more of these ethereal landscapes, notably **New Blue Spring (6)** and **Canary Spring (7)**. Steam rising from these hot springs diffuses the light and gives the terraces—streaked in pastel shades of green, yellow, orange, even pink, and fringed with stony icicle-like stalactites—an alien aspect. In bright overhead light the hot springs are blazing blue, green, and turquoise. Be sure to use a polarizing filter to

Gustav W. Verderber

New Blue Spring

remove the glare on the surface of the pools and saturate the underlying colors. Take your time looking for compositions among the limestone formations through both normal and wide-angle lenses. Use your telephoto lenses to isolate sections of the scene and compose unusual landscape images and bizarre, yet artful abstracts. At New Blue Spring and Canary Spring, it's easy to create images that appear as though they were taken on another planet!

Orange Spring Mound (8)

A popular feature along this road is **Orange Spring Mound (8)**. It's hard to miss; the road skirts this solitary, 30-foot cone within a few feet of its base, from which this formation rises like a miniature volcano. Steam wafts from the top of the cone as a small fountain of boiling, mineral-rich water gushes over the rim and paints the sides in vivid streaks of green, red, and orange. What's more, the colors of the cone change with the seasons, tending toward green in spring and orange in summer, as a progression of various temperature-dependent species of algae replace one another throughout the year! Orange Spring Mound is truly one of nature's dynamic works of art. There's a parking lot and boardwalk in front of the mound from where you can create superbly surrealistic photos of the mound when the early-afternoon sun illuminates the side facing the road.

Old Gardiner Road (9)

Whenever I visited Mammoth, one of my favorite drives was along the **Old Gardiner Road (9)**. At one time this was the only connection between the Mammoth Hotel and Gardiner. It's a twisting, somewhat perilous dirt road that begins, quite unassumingly, at an iron gate behind the Mammoth Hotel and runs (one-way) all the way back to the North Entrance.

As the road climbs high above Mammoth, vast stretches of sagebrush scenery roll away in all directions. Soon there's no sign of civilization other than the dusty road—and even that isn't very reassuring. One can easily imagine riding into Gardiner on horseback, a high-plains drifter, dusty, parched, and sunburned, aching for some shade, a cool drink of water, and companionship. Even when you're in your

Black-billed magpie

car, I urge you to bring along a water bottle and a friend. Gawking at the scenery while driving the Old Gardiner Road is . . . well, let's just say you don't want to end up like a bighorn sheep that lost its footing.

Virtually any time of day, the chances of spotting **pronghorn** grazing in the lush draws off the Old Gardiner Road are extremely high. I've spotted them here at high noon, but for the best light, I would suggest that you travel the road just after sunrise and in the late afternoon. Bring a medium to long (200 to 600mm) telephoto lens.

On the snags—standing dead trees—look for **black-billed magpies**. These large black-and-white birds with very long tails are found throughout the West. Magpies are tolerant birds that, if you approach them casually, will let you get a fine portrait. In direct sunlight their black feathers shimmer like iridescent blackish-green emeralds.

Raven on Orange Spring Mound

Blacktail Plateau (10)

Another good area for pronghorn is along the road between Mammoth and Tower-Roosevelt Junction, especially in the vicinity of **Blacktail Plateau** (10), about 4 miles east of Mammoth. Wherever you see depressions where water pools during a rain and the grasses are a brighter green than they are on the higher, drier areas, that's where you're likely to find pronghorn.

Blacktail Plateau Drive (11)

If you continue east along this part of the Grand Loop Road, you will eventually come to another one-way road, **Blacktail Plateau Drive (11)**. Though not as lofty or as precarious as the Old Gardiner Road, this rugged dirt road gradually lifts you up above the main road to afford sweeping views of the wilderness. Again, for the best light, I would recommend traveling Blacktail Plateau Drive in early morn-ing or late afternoon. Be prepared to stop fre-quently to scan the vistas for landscape com-positions (with a 24 to 50mm lens) as well as for wildlife, including pronghorn and deer.

Grand Loop Road (12)

During your sojourn at Mammoth Hot Springs, consider taking a morning drive south along the **Grand Loop Road (12)** toward Norris Junction. Stretches along this road—especially at **Swan Lake Flats** and **Willow Park**, located a few miles outside of Mammoth—are promis-ing locations for sightings of **moose**, **wolves**, **grizzly bears**, and **coyotes**. Mind you, when I say "morning," I do mean morning—as in dawn.

Swan Lake Flats (13)

Aside from wildlife, an outstanding landscape photo awaits you at **Swan Lake Flats (13)**, where majestic **Electric Peak** points toward

Coyote pair

Gustav W. Verderber

the sprawling western sky. On a calm morning, if you walk a short ways into the meadow, you can find the mountain's gilded reflection on the surface of **Swan Lake** gracing the foreground. Be sure to bring a normal (50mm) to wide-angle (24 to 35mm) lens and your polarizer to add contrast to the reflection and eliminate glare on the water.

Willow Park (14)

If the sun is still too close to the eastern horizon, and Electric Peak is shaded, go check out **Willow Park (14)** a bit farther south, but remember to return here later. At Willow Park the road rises about a dozen feet above an extensive wet meadow and at points commands a convenient, encompassing view of this grassy wetland. Repeatedly "cruising" Willow Park can be very rewarding. **Coyotes** come here to "mouse": hunt for rodents. **Moose,** as much at home in wetlands as in the deep forest, are also spotted here. Grizzly bears come looking for moose or elk but will settle for the more abundant pocket gophers. Solitary wolves are drawn to whatever leftovers they can find, or if they arrive in a pack and are hungry, they will chase down a moose or an elk. It's here that I photographed up close the only wolf I spotted during my nearly four-month assignment in Yellowstone (see page 18).

Whenever you're photographing wildlife, be patient. Those remarkable photos you see in published portfolios in bookstores are the result of many hours spent in the field waiting, observing, and getting to know the animals. To become a good nature photographer, you must learn to be a naturalist. Watch what the animals do. Soon you'll be able to anticipate their movements and be ready the next time your subject displays an interesting behavior. Then you'll have yourself one of those "natural moment images" that all photographers dream about.

Gustav W. Verderber

Cool moose

Sheepeater Cliff (15)

Between Swan Lake Flats and Willow Park, the **Sheepeater Cliff (15)** picnic area is an ideal spot to take a break from the hard work of nature photography and enjoy a snack. Yet this is Yellowstone, after all, and there's hardly a place where the stunning scenery or abundant wildlife doesn't keep you busy creating more images. At Sheepeater Cliff, the jumble of boulders directly behind the picnic tables is a great place to capture a **yellow-bellied marmot** lounging on a rock. At high noon the sun is at your back as you're facing the mound of rocks, banked up here by the last glacier over ten thousand years ago, and the marmots are in their best light. With a medium telephoto, you can actually photograph the marmots from the picnic table while you eat your lunch!

Burned lodgepole stump

II. Madison and Norris Junctions

Approaching Yellowstone National Park from West Yellowstone, the first impression is of a relatively unassuming expanse of arid high plains or sagebrush steppe, crimson sedge bottoms, and willow thickets pinched between steep, forested slopes. Lanky lodgepole pines dress the inclines and ridges, where they seem to grow to order for the very purpose for which various Native Americans used them: framing their tepees or lodges. Hence the name: lodgepole. The landscape is typical of the Northern Range, and though similar to what you may have observed driving south on Interstate 191 from Bozeman, Montana, the scenery is decidedly different.

In contrast to the dramatic, even ostentatious, welcome one receives upon entering Yellowstone through the historic and celebrated North Entrance—passing under the Roosevelt Arch with its lofty inscription and almost immediately confronting the sensational alabaster formations of Mammoth Hot Springs—the West Entrance introduces the park with less flourish but, in my opinion, reveals the true purpose of Yellowstone—the conservation of wilderness—in a more genuine fashion. As you leave West Yellowstone and enter the park, notice the subtle yet profound changes in the surrounding landscape. Stores, gas stations, restaurants, junkyards, telephone poles, billboards, railroad tracks and trains—the bric-a-brac of civilization—all gone. Even the ubiquitous cattle have disappeared from the scene, replaced by roaming herds of elk and bison. In the sky, no low-flying aircraft! In their place, nothing. Just the land, the plants, the animals, and the sky. Indeed, Yellowstone is what it is owing to what it lacks more so than to what the park includes or has to show us by way of stunning attractions like Old Faithful or Mammoth Hot Springs. Welcome to the wilderness, where preservation of our natural heritage—purely for its intrinsic value—is paramount.

A park, by definition, is "a public area of land, usually in a natural state, having facilities for rest and recreation." Clearly Yellowstone National Park exists to fulfill two seemingly paradoxical missions: to preserve some of this country's wild and rugged natural splendor and to provide recreation for millions of visitors who annually flock to the park from all over the world. The challenge, of course, is to strike the proper balance between these two goals.

Overall, Yellowstone National Park has proven to be a model for maintaining a balance between the needs of the public and preserving the wild nature of the Yellowstone ecosystem. Nevertheless, conflicts inevitably arise—sometimes owing to human pressure on the park and sometimes to the forces of nature that push back and reinforce the park's intent to allow nature to pursue its own imperative. Such was the case in 1988 when dangerous **forest fires** raged across nearly 800,000 acres in the park, inciting vehement controversy about whether nature or people ultimately determine the course of events, natural and unnatural, in Yellowstone.

Dramatic evidence of the fires remains throughout the park, especially between the West Entrance and Norris. Mosaics of **burned and unburned forest** reveal the erratic and serendipitous nature of a forest fire. Meanwhile, a new generation of saplings has already begun to fill in the spaces between the blackened and denuded trunks with their fresh, verdant needles reminding us that forest fires are merely another component of the greater Yellowstone ecosystem.

August is typically fire season in Yellowstone. The semiarid climate, high elevation, and warm to hot summers allow dead, dry timber to accumulate in the forest. Storms in late summer and early fall bring lightning, which ignite many of the fires. Yet not all forest fires result from natural causes. Campfires, cigarettes, even sparks from a car's exhaust can and have ignited major forest fires in Yellowstone National Park.

If a fire breaks out during your visit to the park, steer clear of it. Trying to get up close and personal with a forest fire just to grab a few photographs is as foolish as trying to fill your frame with a mother grizzly and her cubs through a 50mm lens! Some of my most stunning forest-fire images were taken miles from the fire. Stay safe, and strive to make the fire part of a landscape composition that provides a sense of scale and reveals the size and extent of the blaze. Show the terrible pillar of black smoke rising and spreading violently like a nuclear mushroom cloud, dimming the sun, casting a menacing pall across the sky. But remember that forest fires are an integral part of the ecology of Yellowstone. In fact, conifers with serotinous cones—like lodgepole pines—depend on fire to help propagate their seeds. Forest fires, therefore, help sustain Yellowstone and the plant and animal species that thrive here.

One such animal species is America's national emblem, the **bald eagle**, which is attracted to the park's abundant water, especially those lakes, rivers, and streams teeming with trout. Approximately 30 nests are scattered throughout the park, typically in tall, dead trees close to water. Thus, be on the lookout for an enormous stick nest whenever you are driving alongside a river or lake. Eagle nests are commonly spotted from the **Grand Loop Road**, along the **Madison River** between the West Entrance and Madison Junction and along the **Gibbon River** between Madison Junction and Norris.

Throughout June and July, you may spot two or three downy eaglets in a nest with binoculars and perhaps one of the adult eagles feeding bits of a freshly caught trout to the ravenous chicks or perched in a tree nearby. During the nesting season, however, you are not permitted to stop your car alongside the road near the nest. So it's best simply to allow someone else to drive you slowly past the nest while you take a photo or two from the passenger window. In certain instances a drive-by shooting is the only way to photograph a subject from the road safely and without violating park rules or bothering your subject. This is when my homemade beanbag comes in handy. I simply roll down my window and drape the beanbag over the door frame, and it provides a soft and steady cushion for my telephoto rig. With good conditions and technique—ample light, a sufficiently fast shutter speed, a firm grip on the camera, and by steadily rather than frantically pressing the shutter button—you'll be delighted with the results. You will need a long telephoto lens, minimally 200mm, and you should arrive in the morning or afternoon when the low-angled sun highlights the faces of the birds.

Madison Information Station (16)

Be sure to stop in at the **Madison Information Station (16)** at Madison Junction. In addition to offering a wide assortment of field guides, maps, and books about the natural and human histories of the park, this station—now a National Historic Landmark that was previously a museum—offers a breathtaking view from the back. Especially in the spring, when Mount Haynes and National Park Peak are still capped with snow and herds of bison and elk are scattered along the Madison River in the foreground to within feet of the back door. In June these herds disperse to other parts of the park. Morning light floods this west-facing view.

Terrace Spring (17)

At Madison Junction the park road diverges; one leg heads south toward the Lower Geyser Basin, and another runs northeastward along the Gibbon River toward Norris Junction. Just north of Madison Junction, the road brushes **Terrace Spring (17)**, a small but lovely hydrothermal area that can be reached from the road via a short boardwalk. Runoff from the spring flows directly under the road into the Gibbon River. A photo here could clearly illustrate the confluence of modern society with the primal forces of nature.

Gibbon Falls (18)

A few miles past Terrace Spring, **Gibbon Falls (18)** is clearly visible on the east side of the road from a turnout overlooking the waterfalls and also provides safe parking as well as a spot for a compelling composition. Plummeting 84 feet, the Gibbon River spills over a remnant of the Yellowstone Caldera—the mouth of the volcano that once formed, and will at some time in the future re-form, all of Yellowstone.

On lightly overcast days, Gibbon Falls receives soft early-afternoon light that will enable you to leave your shutter open for a full second and soften the texture of the water. Slow shutter speeds around 1/2 to 1/8th of a second or longer render moving water as a gossamer stream and give photos a surrealistic impact. I use this effect selectively. In the case of the Lower Falls at the Grand Canyon of Yellowstone I chose to freeze the water with a fast shutter speed (1/125th of a second). In that photo, the texture of the waterfall revealed the sheer volume of water pouring over the brink. Blurring that texture would have removed much of the drama of the photo. So experiment; use both fast and slow shutter speeds to be sure to capture the waterfall with both effects, and make your decision once you see the results. If you find that there is too much light to use a slow shutter speed, use slower film or your polarizer to reduce the exposure by about two stops.

Artist Paint Pots (19)

Some 4.5 miles south of Norris Junction, a small geyser basin offers one of the best opportunities to photograph mudpots: roiling mud also known as paint pots and technically called "solfatares." At **Artist Paint Pots (19)**, a 1-mile loop trail passes under a patch of forest that burned in the 1988 forest fires and leads you to several hot springs and two large mudpots. The advantage of photographing mudpots at this basin is that you can set up your tripod on hard, stable ground rather than a boardwalk, as is the case at **Fountain Paint Pots** in the Lower Geyser Basin (see Section III: Old Faithful and West Thumb). A constant stream of visitors bouncing along on a boardwalk creates annoying camera shake and, consequently, might reduce the quality of your photo. Moreover, crowding the narrow boardwalk with one's tripod is inconsiderate and unsafe.

At Artist Paint Pots you have ample room and a firm foundation for your tripod. If your camera quakes here, it will not be due to the parade of visitors strolling past your tripod but the result of one of Yellowstone's numerous earthquakes. On any given day, Yellowstone experiences frequent tremblers. Most go unnoticed, while some are strong enough to be felt and occasionally rearrange the intricate underground plumbing that feeds water and steam to the geysers. As a result, active geysers periodically stop erupting, or dormant geysers suddenly become active for the first time in years; hot springs appear and disappear; and new fumaroles erupt in the middle of a parking lot!

On a sunny day, a fast shutter speed of 1/500th of a second or faster and a medium telephoto, around 100 to 300mm, will enable you to isolate and capture the motion of a bursting bubble of mud, but you must have quick reflexes. Expose many frames and you will very likely get one or two that are keepers.

Norris Geyser Basin (20)

Speaking of earthquakes, **Norris Geyser Basin (20)** is the most dynamic hydrothermal area in Yellowstone. It is also the hottest, with underground temperatures reaching 459 degrees F. Norris Basin experiences periodic large-scale seismic activity that alters water levels, erup-

Thermophile bands at Norris Geyser

tion cycles, pH, and color throughout the basin. Indeed, features in the basin change daily, and you may be fortunate enough to witness one of these remarkable events as you stroll along the boardwalks among sapphire hot springs, luminous acidic geysers, and pillars of white steam under a cobalt, Rocky Mountain sky.

From the Grand Loop Road on a chilly morning, Norris Geyser Basin resembles a Native American encampment, with columns of steam rising like campfire smoke across the vast basin. For a truly intimate encounter with Yellowstone, arrive early before the crowds. Then you might easily find yourself wandering alone among the caustic cauldrons of bubbling acid (pH around 3.5), inhaling the sulfurous vapors emanating from the hissing fumaroles like dragon's breath, and maybe, just maybe, feeling the earth move. Walking on the wild side of Yellowstone at Norris Geyser Basin is a journey into the Earth's primordial past and dynamic present. Here the menacing geological forces that continue to reshape Yellowstone are just inches under your feet; indeed, it's an unnerving, exhilarating experience.

Use a wide-angle lens to capture this sense of vulnerability. Fill your frame with sweeping views of the hot springs and steam and sputtering geysers, and show the people— disproportionately small and seemingly insignificant—huddled onto the narrow boardwalk, carefully threading their way through this tempestuous basin.

Echinus Geyser (21) and Steamboat Geyser (22)

Unfortunately, the outstanding geysers in the Norris Geyser Basin are also the most unpredictable. **Echinus Geyser (21)** erupts every one to four hours, but if you have the time, it's worth hanging around to watch. Check to see

Gustav W. Verderber

Roaring Mountain

if the pool is full to the point of overflowing. If it is, then Echinus will likely erupt within 20 minutes.

Alas, **Steamboat Geyser (22)**, the world's tallest active geyser, is entirely unpredictable. Intervals between eruptions may last a year or more. Should you be so fortunate as to witness a full eruption, you will see this geyser shoot water 300 to 400 feet into the air, twice as high as the tallest trees. Its steam phase lasts for 24 hours, but good luck!

Roaring Mountain (23)

At Norris Junction, you are within 5 miles of **Roaring Mountain (23)**, an unusual concen-tration of acidic fumaroles and bare, bleached trees scattered across an extremely stark and alien landscape. You can fill your viewfinder through a 50mm lens and capture that sense of austere otherworldliness that the mere mention of "Yellowstone" evokes in our minds. What your still camera will not be able to capture is the very feature for which this hydrothermal basin was named: the roaring sound of the fu-maroles belching steam. Of course, you can also visit Roaring Mountain whenever you are headed north to Mammoth Hot Springs. The fumaroles are located on the west side of the mountain and receive direct sunlight in the af-ternoon. Yet I found the geyserite—the white mineral crust deposited in geothermal basins by the hot water as it evaporates—to be much too bright on sunny days, so I reserved my visits to Roaring Mountain for days when the light was less harsh.

Switching gears from geysers to game, ask almost any visitor to Yellowstone National Park what wildlife they would most like to see in the park, and grizzly bears, wolves, and elk are likely to top the list. Bison are abundant, and to any visitor who spends more than a couple of days in the park, they soon become as ordinary as mosquitoes in a Louisiana bayou and nearly as irritating as they frequently block the road. Bears are always a big hit whenever they are spotted, and wolves are the holy grail for many visitors, which only a lucky few ever get to see and even fewer get to photograph. Yet elk, including regal bulls sporting magnificent crowns of antlers, are numerous enough to provide the average visitor with at least a single sighting or two of one of these majestic icons of the park but not so abundant that they can ever be taken for granted.

A bull's antlers begin growing in April and do not reach their full development until September. The antlers grow very fast, adding upward of a half inch of length daily. As early as July, bulls with awesome, expansive "racks" gather crowds and stop traffic. Which is to say that if you're a typical visitor to Yellowstone arriving during the height of the tourist season in summer, you will not be disappointed if you want to bag yourself a world-class trophy—on film, of course.

Though in summer elk are scattered throughout the park, and you may encounter individuals or small groups almost anywhere, your best chance of seeing herds of elk at that time of the year is along the Gibbon River where it meanders alongside the Grand Loop road between Madison and Norris junctions. Here, the proximity of water and open mead-ows provides an ideal combination for elk to graze and nurse their calves in the relative safety of numbers and where the vigilant herd might more easily spot a predator—notably a wolf or a bear—attempting to sneak up on a defenseless calf. Of course, the situation is also superb for photographing the animals safely from the road. Docile as they seem, it is not safe to walk into the midst of a herd of elk to work individuals at a close distance; an annoyed 500-pound cow defending her calf can kill a man with a single kick. And I have seen a 700-pound bull charge a car and penetrate the passenger door with his antlers.

Once again, the best time to be in the field is early morning. When almost everyone else was queuing up for breakfast, I would be working a bull elk in the first glimmer of golden sunlight with my 300mm telephoto. On cool, misty mornings, whenever a cow yawned or grunted or a bull bugled, you could see the animal's breath. That visible puff of vapor brings a picture to life. Indeed, it's as close as a still photographer can come to recording the sound of nature on film. Once the light turned harsh and the mist cleared, and I had exposed upward of a dozen rolls of film, I drove to the nearest cafeteria for breakfast. By then the lines, if they hadn't disappeared altogether, were short.

In June and July a bull elk's antlers are still covered in velvet. When backlit, the downy fuzz forms a brilliant outline of light around the edges of antlers. At dawn or dusk, this rim lighting gives racks a gilded appearance that is one of the most coveted "special effects" among professional wildlife photographers. It's also a good example of creative exposure—an exception to the rule that the sun must always be at your back.

During early to mid-August, one of the most sought-after photos in Yellowstone is that of a mature bull with tatters of dried velvet hanging from the creamy tips of a formidable new set of fresh antlers that in spots may still be blood-stained where the animal scraped off the dying tissue against a tree. Encountering such a bull is like coming face to face with a victorious gladiator who has just vanquished all of his foes in the Roman Coliseum. The sheer brawn of these superb males, together with their astounding antlers and their combative nature, demands deference—even bears are reluctant to challenge a bull elk in its prime.

In the process of scraping off the velvet, the bulls prepare for battle, polishing and sharpening the tips of their antlers and growing increasingly irascible. By September they are highly aggressive and will fiercely attack anything that annoys them or that they might interpret as a challenge—including photographers carrying their cameras mounted on tripods over their heads and thus resembling young bull elks (with decidedly small racks) foolishly challenging the dominant male in a herd. Welcome to the rut!

The annual rut, or mating season, of the elk in Yellowstone National Park draws visitors, including professional and amateur photographers and natural sound recorders, from all over the world. From the beginning of September through the middle of October, the park echoes with the bugling of bull elk announcing their fitness, the clashing of antlers as bulls challenge and defend their territories and harems, and, if you listen closely, the hum of motor winders. The rut is among Earth's finest natural spectacles, and if you are planning to be in Yellowstone during this season, bring long lenses (a minimum of 200mm), lots of film or backup memory cards, and quick reflexes to catch the action.

Bull elk in velvet with oncoming storm

III. Old Faithful and West Thumb

Yellowstone National Park is one of the most active hydrothermal regions on Earth, home to over 10,000 geysers, hot springs, fumaroles, and mudpots. Indeed, if Yellowstone National Park had little else to offer beyond the numerous geysers and hot springs clustered in and around the Upper, Midway, and Lower Geyser basins, it would still rank among the world's foremost natural wonders. The stretch of the Grand Loop Road between West Thumb and Madison Junction takes you through what is arguably one of the most remarkable landscapes on this planet, where the world's most famous geyser, the largest hot spring in the park, caldrons of boiling mud, screaming fumaroles spewing jets of superheated steam, and herds of bison and elk all compete for your attention.

West Thumb Geyser Basin (24)

I have included **West Thumb Geyser Basin (24)** in this chapter owing to its close proximity (17 miles) to Old Faithful and because it, like most of the park's attractions discussed in this chapter, is principally a geothermal feature. Thus, the techniques I use to photograph the hot springs and geysers around Old Faithful also apply here. Furthermore, I frequently visited West Thumb either at the beginning or end of a day when I had been photographing in the Upper Geyser Basin.

Before venturing into any geyser basin with your camera, make sure you have a skylight filter screwed on over your lens to protect it from the caustic sulphuric acid in the geyser spray. Another precaution—and this may sound

Gustav W. Verderber

Sunrise at West Thumb Geyser Basin

somewhat overbearing—note that the board-walks do not have guardrails. Believe me, it is easy to become so engrossed in your composition that you back up and fall off the edge of the boardwalk. In fact, it is not an uncommon accident in Yellowstone, so please be extra careful.

West Thumb Geyser Basin was among my favorite destinations on cool mornings. If you're looking for that quintessential photograph that captures Yellowstone as the "land of a thousand smokes," then stand on the upper boardwalk at West Thumb at dawn (5:30 AM) when the air is still brisk, and photograph the numerous columns of steam, ascending like smoke from the hot springs and geysers below the boardwalk. Backlit by the sun rising above the silhouette of the **Absaroka Range** and **Lake Yellowstone** in the background, this surrealistic image can only be taken in a few special places on Earth where extensive geyser basins occur, namely Yellowstone, Iceland, and New Zealand.

If you're lucky, you may also see several elk and/or bison huddled in the geyser basin, lured by the warmth of the steam. One morning, I watched a cow elk "dancing" on the geyserite below the middle boardwalk as she repeatedly bumbled into the scalding water that spilled over the rims of the hot springs bubbling all around her. To her and my relief, she eventually bounded over the boardwalk and trotted into the forest to cool her hooves.

Big Cone (25) and Fishing Cone (26)

Follow the boardwalk down toward the lake and along the lakeshore to **Big Cone (25)** and the famous **Fishing Cone (26)**. Fishing Cone gets its name from early visitors to the park who would angle for trout while standing on the rim of the cone. The more sanguine among them would reputedly poach their catches in the spring's scalding water and then eat the poached fish right off of the hook! Clearly this was before the National Park Service established rules and regulations to protect the park's fragile geothermal formations and confined visitors to the boardwalks for their safety. Fishing Cone steaming in the foreground with the sun just peaking above the horizon and lingering patches of ice on the lake in late May or early June is another image that embodies the

Gustav W. Verderber

Big Cone and Yellowstone Lake

primal elements—fire and water—of Yellowstone.

Abyss Pool (27) and Black Pool (28)

At midday, the depths of **Abyss Pool (27)** and **Black Pool (28)** turn brilliant shades of blue. Remember to use a polarizer to remove surface reflections and enhance the colors beneath the surface. The short extension of the boardwalk that juts out toward the west behind Abyss Pool provides a wonderful location for creating a portrait of a companion within a breathtaking landscape. Stand on the platform facing the lake, and have your companion stand on the main boardwalk; Abyss Pool will now occupy the foreground of the scene, your friend or relative will be in the middle ground, and the lake and the mountains will fill in the background. A similar opportunity for a portrait presents itself as you approach the lakeshore and round the corner at Black Pool. In this case the pool and the person—perhaps leaning on the railing and admiring the pool—are the prominent subjects in the foreground, and the lake and the mountains fill in the middle and background respectively.

In the afternoon the sun sets behind your left shoulder as you face the lake from any of the boardwalks at West Thumb. Consequently, everything in front of you—the geyser basin, the lake, and the distant mountains, the latter snow capped in spring and early summer—provide a striking golden contrast against a darkening blue sky.

Twin Geysers (29)

On one occasion I arrived at West Thumb when one of the **Twin Geysers (29)** was erupting. However, by the time I dashed down the boardwalk, the show was over. Of all of my vis-

Gustav W. Verderber

Fishing Cone and Yellowstone Lake

its to West Thumb over the course of the summer, this was the only time I observed an erupting geyser here. Moreover, no geysers at West Thumb are listed in the visitors center as among those whose eruptions are predicted, so this area is certainly not where you want to spend your time waiting to photograph an erupting geyser. For that, you must go to the Upper Geyser Basin.

While at West Thumb, you might consider

taking a brief (15-mile) side trip along the South Entrance road to look for **moose**. Between **Lewis Lake** and the South Entrance, the park road borders the west bank of the **Lewis River** and passes through some of the best moose habitat in Yellowstone. In the summer, bull moose—with spreading racks of velvety antlers—and cows are drawn to the marshes fringing the river where they feed on the succulent aquatic vegetation, slake their thirst, and might even take a cool dip in the lake (moose are capable swimmers). Although I've seen moose here in the middle of the day, to increase your chances, once again I'd recommend early morning or late afternoon.

Upper Geyser Basin (30), Midway Geyser Basin (31), and Lower Geyser Basin (32)

The **Upper Geyser Basin (30)**, **Midway Geyser Basin, (31)**, and **Lower Geyser Basin (32)** are named for their respective locations along the Firehole River. The Lower Geyser Basin is located downstream from the Upper Geyser Basin and the Midway Geyser Basin is—you guessed it—located between the other two.

Kepler Cascades (33) and Lone Star Geyser (34)

Along the way to the Upper Geyser Basin from West Thumb, you will pass **Kepler Cascades (33)** and the trailhead to **Lone Star Geyser (34)** about 3 miles south of the Old Faithful area. If you aren't pressed for time, I recommend stopping to admire the cascades that are located just a few feet from the road. Rather than plummeting over the edge of a precipice, the Firehole River flows gracefully over a series of small ledges in a broad, shallow sheet that forms symmetric patterns of standing rapids on the face of the rocky declivity. If you have a

tripod, use a slow shutter speed (1/2 second or longer) to transform the moving water into ethereal, gossamer ribbons that beautifully capture the grace of the flowing water.

Lone Star Geyser is a 2.5-mile hike one way, so I suggest that you include this geyser in your itinerary only if you have considerable time to spare. Moreover, since Lone Star erupts only once every three hours, you should first consult with the rangers at the Old Faithful Visitors Center to determine the next impending eruption before heading down the trail in hopes of seeing this geyser in action.

Indeed, unless you're prepared to devote a good deal of your stay in Yellowstone to "geyser gazing"—that is, staking out a geyser in anticipation of its next performance—you should first determine which geysers are due to erupt while you are in or near any of the geyser basins, and then arrange your schedule so that you can make the most of your precious time in the park. As I mentioned in the introduction, many of the park's geysers are predictable, and every visitors center will have that day's geyser schedule available. Always drop into the visitors center upon arriving at a geyser basin, and make a note of which geysers are due to erupt while you're there. Now you can incorporate the eruptions into your tour rather than allowing any one geyser to hold you hostage for the better part of a day. After all, some geysers, like Steamboat in the Norris Geyser Basin, are entirely unpredictable and erupt only every few years. You could be in for a very long wait!

Old Faithful Geyser (35)

When you arrive at the Old Faithful Visitors Center, the first geyser you're likely to see steaming, or perhaps even erupting, is also the most famous. About every 90 minutes, **Old Faithful Geyser (35)** faithfully discharges a resplendent white column of boiling water that may reach 180 feet right in front of the visitors center. The eruption may last anywhere from one and a half to five minutes, expelling upwards of 5,000 gallons of water.

Old Faithful can be photographed just about any time of day. My morning preference was to photograph the geyser from in front of the Old Faithful Lodge. (Yes, the lodge is located where it is for a reason.) If you want to get creative, arrive very early, and put Old Faithful between yourself and the rising sun to get a striking backlit scene in which steam appears like smoke, a metaphor for the geothermal forces that power the eruptions.

At midday, the view of Old Faithful from the bleachers in front of the visitor center—in particular from the west end of the bleachers—is ideal. The background is uncluttered and entirely natural, replete with blue sky and dark forest to help emphasize the erupting geyser. Consider the weather forecast when you plan your daily itinerary. Remember that an overcast sky is a poor backdrop for an erupting geyser; the jet of white water shooting from a geyser's vent will basically match the color of the sky, and your photo will lack contrast. It will not be nearly as dramatic as an image of a geyser erupting against a deep-blue sky with a few puffy white clouds filling in the space around the towering pillar of water and steam.

A circular polarizer will help to increase contrast between the white water, the clouds, and the blue sky, but as I noted earlier, at 8,000 feet above sea level, a polarizer may darken the sky too much, rendering it an unnatural navy blue or nearly black. (The effect is even more pronounced on film with a high degree of contrast, such as slide film.) Therefore, while I always carried my polarizer with me, I used it sparingly.

Altogether, the Upper Geyser Basin includes approximately 50 outstanding geother-

mal features. These are all marked on the Old Faithful Trail Guide available at the visitors center. Though I encourage you to see all of the various geysers and hot springs if you have the time, I will confine my discussion of the Old Faithful area to those features that, in my opinion, are the most exciting and compelling from a photographic perspective—in other words, my personal favorites.

Gustav W. Verderber

Old Faithful erupting

Beehive Geyser (36) and view from Firehole River (37)

Although it's one of the most fabulous geysers to watch, **Beehive Geyser (36)** is unpredictable. It erupts twice a day (when active; at times, Beehive experiences periods of complete inactivity), but the exact timing of the eruptions is variable and therefore, cannot be forecast. Still, Beehive will signal when an eruption is eminent; water starts gushing from a small spout alongside the main vent of the geyser within a half hour or so before the main eruption. If you spot that spout spitting, hurry on down to the small array of benches on the south side of the **Firehole River (37)**, just below Old Faithful, for a magnificent view of Beehive. Beehive's vent is cone-shaped and particularly small. Consequently, the water exploding from inside the geyser is squeezed, like water forced through the nozzle of a fire hose, and its trajectory is greatly increased. The result is a roaring eruption of a remarkably straight tower of water that dwarfs the people on the boardwalk. A 50mm lens will frame the Firehole River in the foreground, people standing on the boardwalk beside Beehive for scale, and just the right amount of room in a vertical composition to include the entire geyser, even if the wind spreads some of the fountain into a fantail.

Heart Spring (38) and Lion Geyser (39)

If I were pressed into choosing my favorite composition from among the over 400 images in my Yellowstone portfolio, the image of **Heart Spring (38)** with **Lion Geyser (39)** erupting in the background would certainly be in the top three. Photographers continually strive to distill the essence of a place or subject, and this photograph quite simply embodies one of the most compelling attributes of Yellowstone: its dynamic geology. Indeed, Yellowstone National Park was established, first and foremost, to conserve its unique assortment of geothermal features, not its wildlife nor its vast wilderness. Those were a bonus.

Taken from the boardwalk at its closest approach to Heart Spring, this is a relatively easy photograph to get—provided you're in the Upper Geyser Basin when Lion Geyser erupts. Like Beehive, Lion Geyser erupts roughly twice a day, or about every 8 to 11 hours. However, Lion expels its accumulated volume of water and steam in a series of eruptions that are spaced approximately 1.5 hours apart. So once Lion has entered an eruption phase, it will erupt several times, and all you have to do is ask one of the rangers at the visitors center if Lion has recently erupted. If it has, you'll have at most an hour and a half before the next eruption. Hopefully, that will take place at midday or early in the afternoon, when sunlight ignites the depths of Heart Spring and turns the pellucid, blistering water into a radiant turquoise pool. A polarizer is essential here to remove reflections from the surface of the water that would otherwise diminish the vivid colors emanating from below.

Grand Geyser (40)

If you spot a crowd in a geyser basin, it's usually a clue that a geyser is about to erupt. Although it only erupts about every 10 hours, **Grand Geyser (40)** is so popular that the park service has provided benches to accommodate the hundreds of people who patiently await the eruption of the world's tallest predictable geyser—and arguably the showiest of all of the geysers in Yellowstone. If the benches are filling, I suggest you join the crowd.

Grand Geyser actually consists of a trio of geysers: **Jet**, **Turban**, and **Grand**, which spray

Heart Spring and Lion Geyser

water in powerful bursts at slightly different angles. The result is a spectacular fountain that rises and falls for nearly 15 minutes and may consist of one to four separate eruptions. Reaching 200 feet, the highest burst typically occurs during the second or third eruption, so don't expend all of your film on the initial eruption. Also, in order to include all three geysers in your composition and prevent the top of the fountain from overshooting the upper edge of your frame, use a wide-angle lens—say, around 35mm. Grand Geyser also presents a beautiful rainbow if it erupts in the late afternoon, around 6:00 PM on a clear day.

Castle Geyser (41)

For rainbows, however, nothing beats **Castle Geyser (41)**, provided it, too, erupts anywhere between 6:00 and 8:00 PM. Erupting every 13 hours, Castle's eruptions occur one hour later each successive day so that you can calculate when this geyser will go off and produce a rainbow. If Castle erupts around suppertime on a clear evening, stand next to the interpretive display along the paved walkway southwest of the geyser with the sun behind you and to your left. If you don't see the rainbow from this angle, depending on which way the wind is blowing the spray, keep changing your location until you find the rainbow. You may have to walk a few feet up the boardwalk toward **Crested Pool** to position yourself at the correct angle with respect to the spray before you begin seeing color. Then, wait for the steam phase of the eruption, which occurs about 20 minutes after the geyser begins erupting. It's noisier than the water phase, and the brighter, billowing clouds of steam consist of extremely tiny water droplets that, in turn, reflect considerably brighter and more vivid rainbows.

Even without a rainbow, Castle remains my favorite geyser. The massive cone, the poly-

chromatic mats of thermophyllic algae that extend from the base of the geyser toward the boardwalk, and its stamina—eruptions may last for more than an hour—offer a host of compositions to the creative photographer. I couldn't get enough of Castle Geyser during my stay in Yellowstone; I have over a hundred images of this charismatic geyser in my stock files!

Rainbow over Castle Geyser

Gustav W. Verderber

Riverside Geyser (42)

Riverside Geyser (42), located near the end of the paved trail, about 1.4 miles from the visitors center, is remarkable for its location: It is perched on the bank of the Firehole River. Every six hours Riverside Geyser gives the cool, dark, flowing water in the river a hot shower. The viewing area is from the opposite side of the river, so compositions that combine both the geyser and the Firehole River in the foreground are straightforward. Once again, I opted to capture Riverside Geyser in the evening as the warm light from the setting sun gilded the erupting plume. Yet Riverside receives good light from midmorning onward.

Riverside Geyser

Grotto Geyser (43)

Grotto Geyser (43), just around the bend from Riverside Geyser, spits and sputters almost continuously. Thus, even between major eruptions, which occur every five to eight hours, Grotto can usually be captured spewing water and billowing steam. From the boardwalk you can easily fill your viewfinder with Grotto's surrealistic form with a 50mm lens.

Morning Glory Pool (44)

There are many hot springs in the Upper Geyser Basin, each with its own charm. I mentioned earlier that Heart Spring, combined with an eruption of Lion Geyser, provided me with one of my best Yellowstone images overall. Still, there are two accessible hot springs in Yellowstone National Park that are, quite simply, leagues beyond all the rest. One of them is located at the end of the paved trail in the Upper Geyser basin, roughly 1.5 miles from the visitors center. Not much larger than a kiddie pool, **Morning Glory Pool (44)** is truly one of Yellowstone's most precious jewels.

Like Heart Spring, Morning Glory Pool is best visited in the middle of the day, when the sun reaches deep into the pool, reflects off the white geyserite that encrusts the sides of the vent, and reemerges—sans its long wavelengths at the red end of the visible-light spectrum, which have been stripped away by the water's strong index of refraction—in dazzling shades of blue and green. Communities of thermophyllic bacteria and algae thrive around the shallow edges of the pool, imparting halos of orange and yellow to the crystalline basin. The moment you first lay eyes on Morning Glory Pool, you realize how this remarkable hot spring earned its name.

Again, use a polarizer to eliminate reflections from the surface of the pool. A wide-angle lens, 24mm or shorter, will be necessary

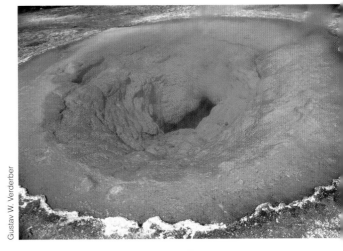

Gustav W. Verderber

Morning Glory Pool

to include the entire pool in your composition from the viewing platform.

Old Faithful Inn (45)

And now for a real point of departure from nature altogether. As a naturalist and nature photographer, I prefer to find my subjects . . . in nature. Unlike most travelers, I typically pass up the generally obligatory snapshots of buildings, cityscapes, statues, monuments, and historical landmarks, preferring instead to seek out the state or national park or wildlife refuge. However, the first time I strolled into the **Old Faithful Inn (45)**, next door to the visitor center, I could not leave until I had taken dozens of photos of that magnificent interior, and on nearly every visit thereafter, I found myself taking additional photos of this architectural masterpiece.

I wanted to capture the warm glow of the interior and the rich tones of the gnarled timbers, so I avoided using a flash. Instead, I balanced my exposure to include both the incandescent lighting and the sunlight streaming in through the windows. To achieve this, I merely stood in the middle of the lobby, took a meter reading

The unique Old Faithful Inn

Gustav W. Verderber

the foreground with large sweeps of these colorful bacterial mats and include a geyser or hot spring in the top of the composition. A medium telephoto will allow you to isolate small patches of the mats and create abstracts of color, texture, and patterns.

Grand Prismatic Spring (48)

I must admit that the first time I visited **Grand Prismatic Spring (48)** in the Midway Geyser Basin, I was awfully disappointed. I had admired some fabulous photos of this hot spring in the bookstore, but all I saw from the boardwalk that skirts the edge of this sprawling, simmering pool was a haze of bluish steam and vast stretches of orange and yellow bacterial mats. It turned out that Grand Prismatic Spring is simply too big to be appreciated from ground level; the photos I had seen were taken from an airplane, which is risky, expensive, and requires a special permit. (The year that I was the Kodak Ambassador in the park, the pilot of a small private plane failed to account for the warmer, and thus thinner, air above the spring. The plane lost lift and plummeted into the geyserite just shy of the pool.)

As I stood on the boardwalk, looking across the hot spring, I noticed a moderately high ridge about a half mile away on the south side of the pool. I returned to my truck, saw that it was close to noon, and so drove south on the Loop Road about a half mile, and pulled into the trailhead for **Fairy Falls (49)**. Then I strapped on my camera bag, slung my tripod over my shoulder, grabbed a granola bar and my water bottle, and started up the dusty trail toward the falls. Above me, the sun was high and relentless. A few scattered cumulous clouds looked like sheep grazing in a cerulean field. Perfect!

Soon I was walking along the foot of the very ridge I had spotted from the boardwalk.

off a neutral gray card that I held up in front of that grand fireplace where light from both aforementioned sources mingled, and then relocated myself at some favorable vantage point on the upper balcony and used a wide-angle lens to encompass as much of the lobby as possible. My exposure, on ASA 50 film, from a tripod, was 1/2 second at F4.

Biscuit Basin (46) and Black Sand Basin (47)

Returning to nature, many more dazzling hot springs and quirky geysers can be found across the loop road from Old Faithful in **Biscuit Basin (46)** and **Black Sand Basin (47)**. To my eye, one of the most attractive features in these two basins are the unique communities of thermophyllic bacteria that create the remarkable bands of dramatic colors along the edges of the pools. A wide-angle lens allows you to fill in

Off to the north, I could see the pastel cloud of blue steam that marked the location of Grand Prismatic Spring. The trail curved around the base of the ridge until, about a mile down the trail, the ridge faced due north. I gulped down half of my water, tepid though it was, and scrambled up the ridge.

I would not allow myself to turn around to glance at Grand Prismatic as I climbed the ridge. That would only spoil the anticipation. It's not a hard climb, just a steep hike to a plateau about 500 feet above the trail, from where, looking north through a gallery of burned lodgepole snags, you can get a clear view of Grand Prismatic Spring. Reaching the plateau, I dropped my pack, took another drink of warm water, and turned around.

From the ridge, I could now see Grand Prismatic Spring in all of its sublime splendor. Eventually one runs out of superlatives to de-

scribe the marvels of Yellowstone. It's easier to describe how I felt as I took in the view from that ridge. I was overwhelmed by wonder. I was dumbfounded. I was transfigured. I cried.

If you attempt this, be sure to pack some water, a snack, and only the equipment you need, leaving most of your photographic armamentarium behind. Bring your camera, a lens or lenses in the range of 50 to 110mm, several rolls of film or a spare card, a polarizer, and your tripod. Hot spring rules apply: Head up on a clear day around noon for maximum color, and reconsider if it's a cool day; too much steam will veil your view of the pool. Oh, and bring a partner to watch for bears; you're off the trail now and fair game. If you do not have a partner, this would be a good time to do like the seven dwarfs: Whistle while you work. Noise usually keeps bears at bay.

Gustav W. Verderber

Grand Prismatic Spring

Firehole Lake Drive (50), Firehole Spring (51), White Dome Geyser (52), and Great Fountain Geyser (53)

Still thirsty for bubbling caldrons and exploding fountains of hot water? Then turn onto **Firehole Lake Drive (50)** just north of Grand Prismatic Spring on the east side of the Grand Loop Road, and follow this short, 2-mile, one-way loop through a fantastic landscape of colossal geysers, violently boiling hot springs, and marvelous scenery.

At the first long turnout on your left, **Firehole Spring (51)** boils incessantly. Menacing white plumes of bubbles churn from deep inside this seemingly fathomless cobalt pool. In the distance **White Dome Geyser (52)** looms above the vast, gleaming plain of geyserite. Typically, White Dome spews forth a relatively short, thin fountain of water every 15 to 30 minutes, but intervals as long as three hours between eruptions are not uncommon.

Just around the bend is the magnificent **Great Fountain Geyser (53)**, another of the predictable geysers. Eruptions of 100 feet occur approximately every 8 to 12 hours and when viewed against the setting sun, they are renowned for their golden splendor.

Fountain Paint Pot Nature Trail (54)

The **Fountain Paint Pot Nature Trail (54)** in the lower geyser basin winds among outstanding examples of fumaroles and paint pots. Leave your shutter open for a second or longer (though be careful not to overexpose the photo on a bright day) to intensify the white steam erupting from the fumaroles. That same superheated, acidic steam dissolves the clay minerals in the ground and liquefies rock, turning it into mud. In the mudpots, the mud—which may be tinted by iron oxides and other colored minerals—bubbles like cooked porridge as steam and water burst through the mire. A fast shutter speed, say, 1/500th of a second or faster, will freeze the bubbles in midburst.

Gustav W. Verderber

Hot spring on Firehole Lake Drive

IV. Fishing Bridge District

Fishing Bridge Village (55)

If your plan is to spend a few days in Yellowstone and venture out to explore the park from one of the park's villages, **Fishing Bridge (55)** is one of the two villages I would urge you to consider. The other is **Canyon Village** (see Section V). In relation to the other districts of the park, both villages are about as conveniently located (a half hour to an hour and a half distance to any other region within the park) as is possible within an area encompassing 2.2 million acres. At Fishing Bridge you're close to Yellowstone Lake, and at Canyon Village you're perched on the east rim of the Grand Canyon of Yellowstone.

Apart from the scenery, another important consideration is the fact that in July and August, the road between these two villages is often jammed with visitors observing and photographing the large herds of bison in Hayden Valley. Bison take full advantage of their right of way in the park and will frequently lounge on the road, bringing traffic to a standstill. Indeed, it could take upward of an hour or two to drive the 10 miles between Fishing Bridge and Canyon Village, especially during the bison rut in August. Thus, if you're visiting Yellowstone during July or August, my recommendation is to stay in Canyon Village while you're exploring the northern half of the park and then move to Fishing Bridge to explore the southern half, or vice versa. Alternatively, if you have more time, you could parcel your stay in Yellowstone over more than two of the park's villages. This would put you within 15 to 30 minutes of all the attractions located within the district in which you were staying.

Admittedly, I have a soft spot for Fishing

American white pelican on Alum Creek

Bridge; it's where I lived during my assignment in the park as Kodak Ambassador. The rangers stationed at Fishing Bridge were among the most superb naturalists and finest individuals I have ever had the pleasure of being with in the field. Their camaraderie helped turn what was already a sublime experience into one of the highlights of my life.

Hayden Valley (56) and Alum (57), Elk (58), and Trout Creeks (59)

I started many of my days in Yellowstone by driving into **Hayden Valley (56)** at the crack of dawn. Both Fishing Bridge and Canyon Villages are gateways to Hayden Valley. The misty landscapes on cool mornings, the creamy early light, and the reflections on the **Yellowstone River**, in particular at **Alum (57)**, **Elk (58)**, and **Trout creeks (59)** offer some of the most marvelous scenery anywhere in Yellowstone. A good sunrise composition is from the famous Fishing Bridge looking downriver.

Bison crossing the Yellowstone River

On a good day in Hayden Valley, you might see a great deal of the wildlife that Yellowstone has to offer. Birds and mammals alike are drawn to the lush wetlands along the Yellowstone River, which meanders through the length of the valley as it flows northward toward the

Grand Canyon of Yellowstone. In early summer the shallows at Alum Creek on the west side of the Loop Road receive glorious early morning light. However, by late summer these wetlands have dried up. At Alum and Elk creeks look for **American white pelicans**, and

might find several **bald eagles**, **osprey**, and **hawks** eyeing the river for cutthroat trout from snags along the shores. **Sandhill cranes** nest in Yellowstone National Park in the summer, and you can often spot the tall, lanky birds feeding in the shallows at Alum Creek and elsewhere along the river. Listen for their reverberating, primeval call.

If you are eager to see and photograph **bison**, there's no better place in my opinion than Hayden Valley. Hayden Valley is known for its large herds, which are typically close to or, as I mentioned above, *on* the road. In the morning, animals on the west side of the road receive the best light. In the afternoon, look toward the river for scenes and subjects richly lit in the ruddy sunlight. Also, look for dramatic silhouettes and backlit subjects.

Bison typically move in a herd, so you can photograph groups of them as part of a landscape scene with normal or even wide-angle lenses. Or you can isolate individuals with short to medium telephoto lenses. Many pullouts along the Loop Road, notably at the south end of Hayden Valley, offer sweeping overviews where one can get an almost aerial view of an entire herd of bison! If you're indeed fortunate enough to see a large herd of these magnificent animals stretching from one side of your viewfinder to the other, you will have captured a part of the west as it was once upon a time.

A spectacle that invariably causes a wildlife (traffic) jam and one that frequently occurs close to the road in Hayden Valley is a herd of bison fording the Yellowstone River. Remarkable to see, thrilling to photograph, is a phalanx of 2,000 pound bison—who, let's face it, were not exactly designed for swimming—confront a river that at its deepest is well over their heads and is at times a raging torrent.

Hesitating momentarily, the herd mills about on the shore, as if deciding whether the grazing on the opposite side is really worth the

a variety of other waterfowl, including **mallards**, **mergansers**, **grebes**, and **Canada geese**. You will need a medium to long telephoto lens to do justice to all but the closest subjects. Birds of prey also come here to feed, and particularly during the salmon run in June you risk of crossing the icy river. Suddenly one of the animals decides that it is and bravely wades into the frigid water, and then another follows, and soon the whole herd boldly plunges into the current. Halfway across, only their heads are visible, their flared nostrils barely clearing the swirling water. You can hear the frantic animals snorting and grunting as they swim laboriously to the other shore. When they reach the other side they emerge, shake off a halo of water, and resume grazing as nonchalantly as a gaggle of geese!

It's not easy for them. Some drown. Others are injured coming ashore, slipping on rocks or clamoring over ledges. Nevertheless, they ford the river frequently, and on any given day, if you're in the right place at the right time in Hayden Valley, you will see the Yellowstone River teeming with horns, bulging eyes, and flaring nostrils.

Though you'll find calves throughout the summer, May and June are best for photographing newly born bison in their rusty spring coats. By summer a calf's coat turns chocolate brown; consequently, they don't stand out from the rest of the herd nearly as well. What's more, spring and early summer offer various opportunities to photograph calves nursing, butting heads, mounting one another, frolicking—in short, displaying their rambunctious nature and preparing for their roles as adults.

Portraits of wildlife are wonderful, but capturing animals behaving and interacting with one another is exceptional and will always result in much more powerful images. Look for bison wallowing in the dust, bellowing, drinking, and, of course, mating. In late July and early August, photographers from all over the world flock to Yellowstone for the first of the two major ruts, or mating seasons. The **bison rut** occurs in August, followed by the **elk rut** in September. (For more on the Elk rut, see Section II, Madison and Norris Junctions.)

By the middle of August, bison have shed their shaggy winter fur. Sleek, trim coats now reveal the true brawn of these immense animals. During the bison rut, feisty bulls single out females approaching estrus and guard the cow until she is ready to mate. Interlopers are met with fierce bellowing, snorting, and, quite frequently, combat. If a dual ensues, a pair of bulls will face each other with lowered heads and glaring, bloodshot eyes. The bulls scrape the ground with their front hooves until one suddenly charges the other. When they collide, the unsettling sound of crashing skulls rings across the valley, and clouds of dust billow up from the dry prairie. Battles are typically brief, so be ready, and anticipate a fight whenever you see a few bulls among a group of cows. Usually one of the combatants relents. On one occasion, however, I observed a bull suffer a serious goring, and the next day we spotted his carcass on the shore of the Yellowstone River.

At any time in Hayden Valley you are likely to spot a **western coyote** hunting in a meadow or loping across a remnant patch of snow. Be prepared to capture the coyote pouncing on a mouse or pocket gopher with a medium to long telephoto lens.

Bison calves

Steam billowing from Dragon's Mouth

Wolves have established packs throughout the park since their reintroduction in the mid-1990s, and though they inhabit Hayden Valley, they are not nearly as plentiful here as in the Lamar Valley. Unless you hear of a reliable sighting of a wolf in Hayden, I would advise you to put off your wolf-spotting efforts until you visit the northern regions of the park.

Mud Volcano (60) and Dragon's Mouth (61)

As for geothermal sites in this region, the only accessible geyser basin in the Fishing Bridge district lies between **LeHardy's Rapids** and **Hayden Valley** at **Mud Volcano (60)**, so-called since it is, in fact, the site of an active volcano. Yet the most photogenic feature in the basin is **Dragon's Mouth (61)**, a hot spring from which

steam billows through a colorful, cavernous opening that Native Americans believed was the origin of mankind. The rising sun shines directly into the cave by 7:00 AM on a clear morning and highlights the striking bands of green and yellow thermophyllic bacteria that grow around the mouth of the "dragon."

Sulphur Caldron (62)

Across the road from Mud Volcano is **Sulphur Caldron (62)**, a large mudpot whose extreme acidity is its most distinguishing feature. Heat and steam percolate up through the porous ground while the acid dissolves the surrounding rocks and soil, creating a sinkhole filled with boiling mud! If you walk a few yards north along the shoulder of the road from Sulphur Caldron and peer through the trees, at the bottom of a steep embankment you'll spot some

Gustav W. Verderber

Gustav W. Verderber

Mudpot bubble at Sulphur Caldron

truly phenomenal mudpots. Here the mud is extremely viscous and forms giant bubbles as it boils. *Do not climb down the embankment!* The gravel is slippery, and if you trip, you may not stop tumbling until . . . Just don't go down the embankment, period. Find an opening in the trees, and safely photograph the mudpots with a medium telephoto from the shoulder of the road.

One of my favorite landscape locations is on the south end of the Sulphur Caldron parking lot. From a ledge looking southward, a 50mm or wide-angle lens will frame a magnificent stretch of the Yellowstone River, herds of bison, and the columns of steam rising from a hydrothermal basin on the east side of the river.

LeHardy's Rapids (63)

Yellowstone's renowned **cutthroat trout** spawn in late June. From Yellowstone Lake, thousands of these dazzling fish swim up the Yellowstone River into the gravely bottoms of its tributaries to lay and fertilize their eggs. You can see, and even photograph them with a medium telephoto from the famous Fishing

Bridge, provided you use a polarizing filter to eliminate surface reflections and arrive on the bridge around midday to assure that the sun is directly overhead, and the fish are receiving maximum light. During peak spawning, you can also watch the fish leaping over a small waterfall at **LeHardy's Rapids (63)**, just south of Hayden Valley. You'll need quick reflexes and a shutter speed of at least 1/1000th of a second to freeze the motion of a trout soaring over the falls. Also at LeHardy's Rapids, look for **American white pelicans** fishing in the rapids and gliding low over the river. LeHardy's is a good place to catch these distinctive birds in flight with a long telephoto lens.

Behind the Fishing Bridge Visitor Center, the lakeshore offers grand views of Yellowstone Lake and the Absaroka Range in the distance. American white pelicans cruise very close to the shoreline, especially if someone is fishing. The birds are bold and will attempt to grab a fish as it's being reeled in or the moment that it's released, so you can get frame-filling images of pelicans here with a short telephoto lens if you position yourself close to someone who is fishing. In the spring both male and female pelicans sport the distinguishing "centerboard" on the upper bill, which they shed by July. As you face the lake, the sun will rise above the treetops around 8:30 and then be directly behind you in the morning, bathing the pelicans in soft, warm light. Be sure to underexpose these very bright birds if they are indeed receiving direct sunlight by about one stop, as you would any extremely bright subject in full light.

Pelican Valley (64)

Just east of the visitors center on the Loop Road is **Pelican Valley (64)**. On a clear day the marsh at the mouth of Pelican Creek is a good place to photograph silhouettes of birds, including sandhill cranes and American white pelicans, as well as brilliant reflections in the morning and afternoon. The marsh is too broad, however, to offer good close-up opportunities of the wildlife, unless you're extremely lucky.

Grizzly bears frequent the low elevations from the time they emerge from hibernation to the middle of summer. When the weather warms in July, they retreat to the high country, so bear sightings from the Grand Loop Road become scarce in midsummer. Grizzly sightings are most common from early May through June in Hayden Valley and especially in the Fishing Bridge area during the trout run. Bears often follow the shore of the Yellowstone River and pass directly underneath Fishing Bridge searching for migrating trout! In Pelican Valley, grizzlies are so numerous in the spring and early summer that the trail into the valley is closed until the fourth of July. In fact, from Fishing Bridge to Sylvan Pass such an ideal combination of ecosystems (lake, river, and terrestrial) occurs that this stretch of the East Entrance road provides some of the most outstanding bear habitat in the park and, in turn, offers superb opportunities to safely see and photograph grizzly bears at extremely close range.

As I mentioned earlier in this guide, the road between Fishing Bridge and Sylvan Pass is squeezed between the lake and a low ridge. So whatever wildlife you may encounter while driving through this corridor will necessarily be found somewhere between the ridge and the lake, which are, on average, no more than 500 feet apart. Put your car in the middle of that distance, and anything you see will have to be within 250 feet of your car. Or closer! Though the road runs generally west to east, it slants slightly northwest to southeast. Consequently, the afternoon rather than the morning light tends to be better on the side opposite of the lake, where you're more likely to see grizzlies grazing along the grassy ridge. Thus, as I indi-

cated earlier, my favorite time to "cruise" for grizzlies here was after dinner, from about 7:00 to sunset.

As long as you remain in your car, you will not be violating any park rules, even if the bear decides to cross the road and pass within inches of your bumper. A medium telephoto and some persistence will bring you frame-filling photo opportunities of Yellowstone's famed grizzlies.

As you drive along the East Entrance road, keep an eye out for **yellow-bellied marmots** lounging on the lichen-covered ledges on the side of the road opposite the lake. They are especially common in the areas of **Mary** and **Sedge bays** or wherever there are rocky outcroppings. I frequently spotted them soaking up the last rays of the setting sun in the late afternoon and early evening. If you're patient and stealthy, you can approach them with a medium to long telephoto lens. As my friend Bob Green-

Yellow-bellied marmots

Gustav W. Verderber

burg demonstrated, talking to these skittish cousins of the groundhog soothes them, and they will reward you with some fine portraits in return for a bit of engaging conversation.

Lake Butte Overlook (65)

A few miles east of Pelican Valley look for a sign marking the road up to **Lake Butte Overlook (65)**. Follow the road to the top of **Lake Butte** and enjoy what is truly the most popular view of Yellowstone Lake. On a clear day, one can even see the magnificent **Grand Tetons** far off in the southwest. I preferred visiting Lake Butte in the afternoon, when the sun was on the Tetons, though both morning and afternoon offer strong landscape possibilities.

Sylvan Pass (66)

If you drive all the way up into **Sylvan Pass (66)**, look for bighorn sheep and mountain goats. Though both of these species are rarely spotted here, the thrill of seeing a goat or a sheep perched precariously on an overhang is worth the minute or two it takes to grab the field glasses and scan the slopes and ledges for these elusive animals. In the spring and early summer, blooms of **high-elevation wildflowers**, including lupine and Indian paintbrush, adorn the roadsides near Sylvan Lake. You'll need some extension tubes or a macro lens to isolate individual plants, or a use a normal or wide-angle lens to include a patch of flowers in a landscape composition.

Yellowstone Lake Hotel (67) and Gull Point Drive (68)

The Loop Road between Fishing Bridge and West Thumb hugs the shoreline of Yellowstone Lake. Along the way, numerous pullouts accommodate splendid views of the lake and the **Absaroka Range**. As one might expect, the

Gustav W. Verderber

view of the lake and these majestic mountains is especially remarkable from the terrace of the grand **Yellowstone Lake Hotel (67)** at Lake Village. West of the hotel, at Bridge Bay, **Gull**

Grand Tetons from Lake Butte Overlook

Point Drive (68) leads to a picnic area and a marshy, east-facing shoreline on Yellowstone Lake that presents exceptional sunrise compositions replete with awe-inspiring reflections (on a calm day) at dawn. Early in the morning I frequently spotted **mule deer** in the clearings on my way to photograph the sunrise at West Thumb.

Grand Canyon of Yellowstone

V. Canyon

Grand Canyon of Yellowstone (69)

Yellowstone's legacy of fire and ice is magnificently manifested in the breathtaking Canyon area of the park. Here volcanism and glaciation collaborated to form what, in my view, ranks among the wonders of the world. Approximately a half million years ago, rhyolite, a dense, volcanic lava, partially covered a thermal area immediately west of the canyon. Heated steam and gases from this geothermal cauldron altered and weakened some of the rhyolite. Then about 14,000 years ago the Wisconsin glacier, and subsequently its meltwaters, carved and eroded away the weakened rhyolite, leaving behind a 20-mile-long gorge that varies from 800 to 1,200 feet deep and 1,500 to 4,000 feet wide, which we know today as the **Grand Canyon of Yellowstone (69)**. The Yellowstone River courses through the canyon like a long braid of emerald jewelry draped across a gold-and-bronze sculpture.

Where the hard, unaltered rhyolite that prevailed against the weathering of the thermal activity and the abrasion of the glaciers meets the softer, eroded rhyolite, tall precipitous cliffs tower over the canyon. The Yellowstone River plummets over two such seams, forming the Upper and Lower Falls. I have had the good fortune of visiting and photographing a great deal of this planet, from the arctic to the Galapagos Islands. Yet when I first approached the edge of the Grand Canyon of Yellowstone at Artist Point and beheld the Lower Falls early one morning in May of 2003, I was overwhelmed. It was easily among the most magnificent scenes I have ever seen, let alone photographed.

Canyon Village (70), Artist's Point Overlook (71), and Lower Falls (72)

In the vicinity of **Canyon Village (70)**, the canyon runs roughly northeast to southwest. Standing at **Artist Point Overlook (71)** at the terminus of the south rim drive and facing the **Lower Falls (72)** plummeting 308 feet (higher than Niagara Falls) over its precipice of volcanic rock about a mile upstream, the sun rises to the right and behind the observer. Thus, the Lower Falls receive rich, early-morning light once the sun clears the north rim around 7:30 AM during the spring and summer months. A warming filter helps retain the yellow hues of the rhyolite, which may have been what led the Minnetaree Indians to name the Yellowstone River after the rocks that contain it. (It is a common misconception that Yellowstone [the river as well as the park] was named for the yellow stone in the canyon. Though the Minnetaree named the river, they inhabited eastern Montana, where they may or may not have observed similar yellow hues in the bluffs along the banks of the Yellowstone. Subsequently, French Canadian fur trappers encountered the Minnetaree and learned of the river's name. In point of fact, the park was named after the river that runs through it, not the vivid yellow hues of the canyon walls.) If you prefer the falls to appear realistically crisp in your photo—that is, if you want the water plunging over the edge of the rim to retain the same texture that you perceive with your eyes—then use a shutter speed of 1/125th of a second. Slower shutter speeds soften the texture. Faster shutter speeds render the water even crisper; indeed, they

Gustav W. Verderber

Lower Falls with a rainbow

make the falls appear sharper than our eyes actually perceive it to be.

While my preference was to capture the Lower Falls completely bathed in early-morning light, I have seen stunning photos of the Lower Falls taken while the waterfalls were still shaded by the north rim. The oblique sunlight creates a dizzying pattern of light and shadow on the canyon walls that, if framed properly, can result in very dramatic photos. The compositions from Artist Point, with medium, long, and wide-angle lenses—without even

from sunrise to shortly after 10:00 AM. The play of highlights and shadows and the saturation of the various colors imparted to the canyon walls by the oxidation of minerals in the rhyolite, from bronze to gold to ochre, are a moveable feast of compositions that will thoroughly engage you in the art of nature photography for several hours.

Should you continue to doubt my opinion that the scene of the Lower Falls from Artist's Point ranks among the Earth's natural wonders, be sure to be at Artist Point Overlook on a clear morning at precisely 9:45. I'm certain you'll be convinced.

At that exact moment, the cloud of mist at the bottom of the falls turns luminous as though lit from within by the northern lights. Imperceptibly at first, a cast of purple appears at the top of the cloud. After a few minutes the color is striking as the purple band slowly slides down the mist toward the north side of the river, and behind it, bands of green, yellow, and orange appear. By 9:55, the mist at the foot of the Lower Falls has become a complete, shimmering rainbow! When one considers the confluence of elements necessary to produce this remarkable phenomenon—the angle of the sun, the orientation of the river, the ledge, the waterfalls, the volume of water—I believe few would argue that the Lower Falls of the Grand Canyon of Yellowstone National Park between 9:45 and 10:00 AM is indeed one of the most glorious scenes on Earth.

To capture this colorful event on film, you need to use slow, color-saturated film. Fast film tends to reduce saturation, and the subtle hues of the rainbow will appear pale and unremarkable. Also, I found that a circular polarizer helps to concentrate the colors.

While the falls are clearly the main attraction, don't neglect the canyon itself. Look downstream from the overlook. In the afternoon, when the sun circles around toward the

once moving your tripod—are multitude and limited only by your imagination and patience. Which is why I highly recommend devoting at least one sunny morning of your sojourn in the canyon area to a visit to Artist Point so that you might experience an entire morning there, southwest, you may want to return to capture abstract landscapes of the canyon formations gilded by the setting sun.

Upper Falls (73) and Uncle Tom's Overlook (74)

The **Upper Falls (73)** are best viewed from the **Uncle Tom's Overlook (74),** also on the south rim of the canyon. At 109 feet, the Upper Falls are neither as tall as the Lower Falls nor the centerpiece of the grand vista of the canyon that frames the Lower Falls. Yet as waterfalls go, they are still spectacular. The Upper Falls are picturesquely framed by lodgepole pines and also sport a fabulous rainbow at around 8:00 AM from June through July. By the beginning of August, the sun's angle is too low for sunlight to reach the bottom of the waterfalls, and the rainbow disappears.

Uncle Tom's Trail (75) and South Rim Trail (76)

For the intrepid visitor up for a bit of adventure and keen on probing the depths of the canyon, the **Uncle Tom's Trail (75)** descends steeply to a small landing perched about three quarters of the way down the south wall. From here the Lower Falls are so close, you can literally feel the power of the Yellowstone River spilling over the lip of the north rim. And here again a rainbow appears between 8:00 and 9:30 AM in the white plume of mist at the foot of the falls. Should you endeavor to make this arduous climb, however, take along only your camera, a light tripod, normal (50mm) and wide-angle lenses (if you have a zoom lens spanning 24 to 50mm, all the better), a polarizer, and your film or memory cards. Jettison all your other paraphernalia, and pack lots of water and some snacks. Most of the trail actually consists of a staircase, similar to a fire escape—with 300

steps making a vertical drop of 500 feet! Needless to say, the easy part is the descent. Give yourself at least twice as much time to climb back up than you took going down, and take frequent breaks. Remember, you're at 8,000 feet above sea level.

If you are not in good physical condition, don't bother with the Uncle Tom's Trail. This is not the most appealing view of the Lower Falls, and there is little to see along the way. The trail is hemmed in by forest and ledge on either side—and, besides, you're too busy watching your footing and avoiding people huffing and puffing their way back up the trail to enjoy the occasional glimpse of the canyon from the staircase.

Instead, for views of the canyon, stroll the **South Rim Trail (76)** from the Wapiti Trailhead to Uncle Tom's parking lot and beyond, if you wish, all the way to Artist Point. The easy 1.75-mile trail parallels the canyon as it snakes among the pines and skirts the precipice, where it affords stunning overviews of the canyon and the falls.

To get away from the crowds and experience more of the wilderness, I recommend the 1-mile trail from Uncle Tom's parking lot to **Clear Lake.** Along this stretch of backcountry, you're likely to encounter grizzly bears so be careful and hike with a group of three or more people.

Lookout Point (77)

Lookout Point (77) on the north rim of the canyon affords yet another view of Lower Falls. From here also, the rainbow on the falls appears around 9:30 AM. Admittedly, this was my second favorite overlook for photographing the rainbow. The colors intensify as the rainbow creeps from the south bank of the river across to the north side, so don't waste a great deal of film until the rainbow appears to be in line with the river itself. That's when the colors will be most brilliant. If you have only one morning to spend in the canyon area, visit both overlooks prior to the rainbows' scheduled appearances, and choose your favorite location.

Red Rocks Point (78)

Like the Uncle Tom's Trail, the path leading down the north wall of the canyon to **Red Rocks Point (78)** (which forks off the short trail from the parking area to Lookout Point) is an arduous climb. Though not quite as steep, it's still a formidable walk back up. However, many photographers favor the view of the Lower Falls and its rainbow, which also appears here at 9:30 AM, from the platform at Red Rocks Point over all the others. You will need a normal to slightly longer than normal lens— say, 50mm to 100mm—to frame the falls without including the tops of nearby trees in the foreground. Or if you cannot eliminate the trees from your composition, be sure to use a small aperture, F11 or smaller, so that the trees are not terribly out of focus. Soft (blurred) foreground objects nearly always detract from a composition.

North Rim Trail (79)

Along the short stretch of the **North Rim Trail (79)** between the Grandview parking lot and Lookout Point you will get a close-up view of some of the canyon's most outstanding geologic sculptures. **Bald eagles**, **ravens**, and **osprey** soar over a breathtaking landscape of lofty pinnacles and sheer cliffs. Upward of seven pairs of osprey nest in this area of the canyon between early May to late August. Scan the tops of the rocky spires and the lips of overhanging ledges with binoculars for the large stick nests in which you might spot a clutch of eggs or brood of mottled-brown nestlings.

Mule deer on Cascade Lake Trail

Gustav W. Verderber

Extremely long telephoto lenses of at least 800mm are necessary to photograph these lofty and distant nest sites.

Grandview Point (80) and Inspiration Point (81)

Grandview Point (80) and **Inspiration Point (81)** provide outstanding views of the canyon and the Yellowstone River, as does the stretch of the North Rim Trail between these two lookouts. Before noon, both views tend to be into the light, but by 3:00 PM the sun has swung around to the southwest side of the canyon, highlighting the rich earth tones of the south rim and the contrasting green ribbon of the Yellowstone River coursing wildly through this magnificent corridor on its way to the Missouri River and eventually, the Mississippi River. Use telephoto or zoom lenses to isolate rock forma- tions and create abstract compositions and medium to wide-angle lenses for sweeping landscapes.

Cascade Overlook Trail (82)

If you're hungry for more overviews of the canyon, stroll along the **Cascade Overlook Trail (82)** eastward from the **Glacial Boulder** (on the North Rim Drive at the entrance to the turnoff to Inspiration Point). Very dramatic views of the canyon and the Yellowstone River are within a half mile of the boulder. The Glacial Boulder, by the way, is an enormous rock plucked out of the Beartooth Mountains and dropped on the edge of the canyon around 10,000 years ago by the last glacier.

Brink of the Lower Falls (83) and Brink of the Upper Falls (84)

For especially dizzying perspectives, the trails to the brinks of the Upper and Lower Falls will lead you to the edges of both waterfalls, where you can peer straight down the full length of these immense torrents. The trail to the Brink of the Lower Falls (83) is another very steep, winding trail that descends 600 feet down the face of the north wall of the canyon and is not recommended for anyone who is not in good physical condition. On the other hand, the trail to the **Brink of the Upper Falls (84)** is much shorter and not nearly as steep. Rain- bows are commonly seen from the Brink of the Upper Falls whenever direct sunlight reflects off unusually large bursts of spray that occa- sionally erupt from the bottom of the water- falls. In the spring a beautiful, ephemeral waterfall can be viewed from the short trail be- tween the Brink of the Upper Falls and the Chittenden Bridge.

Cascade Lake Trail (85) and Cascade lake (86)

Clearly, the chief attractions in this part of Yellowstone National Park are the Grand Canyon of Yellowstone and the Upper and Lower Falls. Nonetheless, they are not the only

Twilight over Cascade Lake

reasons for devoting at least a couple of days to this area of the park.

From Canyon Junction, the Grand Loop Road climbs over Dunraven Pass toward Tower-Roosevelt. If you're in the mood for a short hike across flat, easy terrain, then I highly recommend the **Cascade Lake Trail (85)**, which begins at a trailhead on the west side of Dunraven Pass about 1 mile north of Canyon Junction. Initially passing through lodgepole forest, the trail eventually breaks out into sweeping meadows where you are sure to spot bison and likely to encounter moose, grizzly bears, and even wolves and that are adorned with wildflowers in June and July. The impact of the 1988 forest fires is evident from the trail; notice the contrast between the rich green unburned forest and the ghostly gray patches of the burned forest. The trail eventually arrives at pristine **Cascade Lake (86)**, about 2 miles from the trailhead, and then continues westward another 5 miles, until it emerges at a second trailhead near **Norris Junction**.

Burn patterns and Mount Washburn

Gustav W. Verderber

Mount Washburn Trail (87) and Mount Washburn (88)

After spending my mornings photographing in the Grand Canyon area, I would often enjoy a late breakfast at the Canyon cafeteria and then spend the middle of the day photographing the wildflowers and views along the **Mount Washburn Trail (87)**. A little under halfway between Tower-Roosevelt and Canyon Junction, the Mount Washburn Trail leads from the Loop Road to the pinnacle of **Mount Washburn (88)**.

The trail climbs very gradually for roughly 3 miles to the summit, but it's certainly not necessary to hike the entire trail to enjoy its many charms. Within sight of the trailhead, garlands of **wildflowers** line the trail in June and July and **golden-mantled ground squirrels** strike perky poses on the lichen-encrusted ledges only a few feet from the north side of the trail, where the southerly angle of the sun shines on them as perfectly as a studio light. If you decide to venture up to the summit, during your ascent and descent, keep an eye out for **bighorn sheep** and for **black** and **grizzly bears** in the meadows below the trail. A good zoom lens in the 80 to 100mm range for the wildlife, a wide-angle lens for the scenics, plus a macro lens or a kit of extension tubes for the wildflowers will keep the load light.

From the summit the view of Hayden Valley and the chasm that is the Grand Canyon of Yellowstone are unparalleled. The rim of the 40-mile wide Yellowstone Caldera—the remnant of the active volcano (relax; eruptions occur roughly every 640,000 years) that Yellowstone is perched atop and accounts for the extensive geothermal activity that has made the area famous—is also clearly visible as a low, forested ridge to the southeast.

Chittenden Road (89)

Just north of the Mount Washburn trailhead, look for the **Chittenden Road (89)**, a gravel road that turns sharply southeast off the main road. Grab your telephoto (200mm or more) and stroll along the road. If you're fortunate, you'll glimpse a flash of the most brilliant blue you can imagine. That was a **mountain bluebird!** This relatively scarce species has a spotty distribution, owing to its attraction to burned and otherwise disturbed forests such as clearcuts and avalanche clearings. Yellowstone's susceptibility to fire helps maintain suitable habitat—open, shrubby areas—within the park and, in turn, helps sustain a thriving bluebird population.

Keep your eye on the bird. Eventually it will perch on a low bush, perhaps to feed on an insect it has just caught, and if you're patient and move slowly, you'll soon have one of these resplendent birds within range.

Otter Creek Picnic Area (90)

The **Otter Creek Picnic Area (90)** just south of Canyon Junction is a beautiful location for views of the Yellowstone River, especially at sunrise when the river is veiled in morning mist. Pelicans gather here, so be patient. Rather than just a static landscape photograph, you may get a dynamic composition of the river draped in amber, early-morning fog with a flotilla of pelicans in the foreground. Some mornings I came here, set up my camera on a tripod with a 50mm lens focused on the river, and sat on the picnic bench with my coffee mug, content to see what might swim through my viewfinder. The woods and meadows around the picnic area are also the favorite haunts of the elusive and largest of all owls, the **great gray owl**.

Just west of Canyon Junction, along the stretch of road between Canyon and Norris,

look for **moose** in the draws and wetlands early and late in the day. **Elk** become more common as you head west from Canyon toward Norris and Madison but are often seen grazing in the meadows or lounging in the shade of the forest in the immediate vicinity of Canyon Junction. During my assignment in the park, three prime bulls, nicknamed the "Boys of Summer," sojourned at Canyon Junction throughout the season. I thus had the wonderful opportunity to capture these splendid animals with their nascent antlers still swathed in velvet and again shortly after they had shed this soft, sustaining covering to reveal the magnificent antlers that were still stained dark red by the blood that had nourished their growth since the spring.

Gustav W. Verderber

Bull elk after shedding velvet

VI. Tower-Roosevelt and the Lamar Valley

Dunraven Pass (91)

The Grand Loop Road through **Dunraven Pass (91)**, especially the stretch between the Mount Washburn trailhead and Tower Falls, affords some of the most spectacular vistas in Yellowstone. Breathtaking views of the high-plains landscape typical of the arid Yellowstone plateau become more and more frequent as the windy, vertiginous road ascends the southern flank of Mount Washburn, crests at nearly 9,000 feet above sea level, and then descends toward Tower Fall. Turnouts along the road provide ample opportunities for landscapes, including the mosaic of burned and unburned forest, a legacy of the famous **1988 forest fires**.

Take a moment at the turnouts to scan the broad meadows below the road for **grizzly** and **black bears**. Both species are frequently spotted along the north side of Dunraven Pass, particularly in the morning and afternoon. In most instances, the bears are too far for even the most powerful lenses to reach. Still, a wild bear impels us to pause and savor the moment, if only to acknowledge the idea of wilderness and appreciate its realization. This is, after all, what Yellowstone is all about, and we should never become so intent on getting images that we don't bother to stop and simply marvel over the sublime wonders of the park or the intrinsic value of wild nature.

Tower Fall (92)

Among the most whimsical features in the park, **Tower Fall (92)** is a fanciful landscape of austere pinnacles that brings to mind the towers of a fairy-tale castle, hence its name. It's as if the geologic processes that sculpted the an-cient volcanic rock—namely, eruptions, glaciation, wind, and water—contrived to create a sand castle. Then, as any child (or any adult who knows enough to sustain their inner child) is apt to do, these playful forces carved a streambed and let Tower Creek flow through their imaginative construction. Not satisfied, they added a 132-foot waterfall replete with a beautiful rainbow!

Located about 2 miles south of the Tower-Roosevelt Junction, the trail to the bottom of Tower Fall begins at the parking lot and drops steeply into the gorge. It's a half mile to the bottom of the waterfall, so again remember to lighten the load and pack only the necessary equipment, ample water, and a snack. Stand a bit downstream of the falls, and during the summer on a clear day, a rainbow will arch across the waterfall at around 8:00 AM. You can create a compelling composition with a normal 50mm lens.

Hexagonal Columns (93)

Just beyond Tower Fall, if you look across the Yellowstone River, you will see another striking geologic formation—more handiwork by those wild and crazy geologic forces. Tall **hexagonal columns (93)** form a thick layer in the cliff face on the opposite side of the river. You are looking at an ancient lava flow. It's solidified, of course, and composed of basalt that, due to the crystalline structure of the mineral, cracks into these six-sided columns whenever it cools and hardens very slowly. The cliff faces west, so I'd recommend photographing the columns early in the afternoon, when the sun begins to illuminate them at an oblique angle and creates a thin shadow along one side of

Gustav W. Verderber

Full moon over the Lamar Valley and pronghorn

each of the columns. This helps accentuate their unique, angular profile.

Calcite Springs Overlook (94)

Be sure to pull over at the **Calcite Springs Overlook (94)**, about 1 mile north of Tower Fall. **Bighorn sheep** are often spotted on the cliffs across the river opposite of the overlook. Scour the precipice carefully with binoculars since the buff-colored sheep blend into the rocks and soil extremely well, and it takes a keen eye to spot one lounging on a ledge. In the spring and early summer, you may be fortunate enough to spot a group of rams and ewes huddled in a shady grove just off the road, but as

the season progresses the sheep move to the high, rocky country with which they are more typically associated.

While scanning the rock face for sheep, you might also spot a family of **peregrine falcons**. The narrow, recessed ledges are ideally suited for raising a brood of chicks out of harm's way of most predators. Once severely endangered by the overuse of pesticides, in particular DDT, peregrine falcon populations are recovering nationwide. They've done so well that in 1999, the birds were removed from the endangered species list. In Yellowstone alone there are upwards of 20 nesting pairs!

Both the sheep and the falcons would require very long telephoto lenses to do them justice in a photograph. You'll need a minimum of 600mm to get identifiable images of the sheep and upward of 1000mm to reveal that those fuzzy things huddling under an overhanging ledge are indeed peregrines.

At Tower-Roosevelt Junction, turn west toward Mammoth Hot Springs, and take a brief 2-mile side trip to see one of Yellowstone's **petrified trees**. Ancient volcanic eruptions and mudflows buried vast forests in Yellowstone. While they were buried, groundwater leached into the spaces within the wood and deposited silica (quartz), turning the trees into stone. Wind and water have subsequently eroded the overlying sediments, exposing many of the trees. This is one of the more accessible specimens, an ancient redwood. There are many more on the aptly named **Specimen Ridge**, located at the top of the ridge along the Northeast Entrance Road, together with superbly preserved leaves, microscopic pollen, and conifer needles.

Early one sparkling morning, Dan Stebbins, one of the interpretive rangers, and I turned the corner at Tower-Roosevelt Junction and headed into the Lamar Valley well before sunrise. The moon was full, and the Lamar River shimmered under a diaphanous curtain of mist that draped the pewter surface of the river for as far as we could see down the valley. We passed dark, scattered mounds of bison dozing in the chill air and the occasional pronghorn, pale and ghostly in the blue-white moonlight, placidly grazing on the dewy grass.

Dan and I were hoping to catch a glimpse of the Druid Peak pack. Most mornings during my sojourn in Yellowstone, this pack of **gray wolves** would venture from their den at the base of Druid Peak, cross the road—sometimes within feet of the photographers and visitors who were lucky enough to be in the right place at the right time—bound across the river, and

set forth to spend the day in the woods on the far side of the valley. There they would hunt, socialize, and teach their cubs all the things a gray wolf needs to know about surviving and once again being part of the Greater Yellowstone Ecosystem.

By preying on weak and sick individuals and thereby helping to sustain the vigor of their prey species—principally **elk**, **pronghorn**, **deer**, and **small mammals**—and by providing leftover food bonanzas for ravens, bears, foxes, and other scavengers, the gray wolf was once a valuable predator that played a vital role in this country's ecology. Yet the survival of early settlers depended on their ability to raise livestock and hunt game—elk and deer—which put them in direct competition with wolves for food. Predators like wolves, bears, cougars, and coyotes were removed to allow game species to thrive. Greed, thoughtlessness, and a view of natural resources as an inexhaustible bounty took their toll. Eventually, even valued game populations were reduced to critical numbers. (Consider that upward of 60 million bison once roamed from the Pacific to the Appalachians!) As their natural prey became scarcer and scarcer, wolves began raiding stockyards and killing sheep and cattle, providing ranchers with even more incentive and justification to shoot, poison, and otherwise exterminate the wolf and make the country safe for cows and sheep. Originally ranging throughout most of North America, wolves had been virtually eliminated from the contiguous 48 states by the early 1900s. Scattered populations survived in a few northern states and Canada.

As our understanding of ecology grew, however, we became aware of the interconnectedness of species, the concept of niches, and the important role that every plant and animal plays with respect to maintaining the equilibrium and health of their respective ecosystems. In the 1970s our burgeoning environmental awareness led to the enactment of the Endangered Species Act, which mandated, among other things, that wherever possible, the U.S. Fish and Wildlife Service restore species that had been eliminated. In 1974 the gray wolf was listed as an endangered species, and recovery of the wolf wherever a viable population could be established was thus required by law. As most of the components of the gray wolf's preferred habitat were still intact in Yellowstone, notably, viable prey populations, extensive wilderness, and minimal human intrusion, the park was chosen as the most likely location where a restoration plan would have the greatest chance for success.

Following extensive planning, controversy (farmers and ranchers, in large part, still oppose the idea of wolf restoration), and public hearings, a total of 31 wolves were captured in Canada and released in Yellowstone and central Idaho between 1994 and 1996. As of March, 2003, some 273 wolves live in 30 packs in the greater Yellowstone area. Of these, 14 packs—comprising 148 wolves—live within the park.

An average pack of gray wolves includes 8 to 10 highly socialized animals. Each pack consists of two leaders, an alpha male and female, and the individuals each have their own personality, traits (color phases include black to gray), and disposition. The pack commands a territory ranging from 18 to 540 square miles and is maintained by urine scenting and vigorously defended against intrusion by other wolves. Wolves are extremely elusive, clever, and intelligent animals. Too see a wild wolf is a privilege. To capture a wild wolf on film is, to use a cliché, a genuinely spiritual experience.

The morning that Dan and I went in search of wolves, we were not sufficiently privileged to spot any members of the Druid Pack. However,

A wolf in the Lamar Valley

on another morning, near the end of my Yellowstone assignment, I was returning from Mammoth Hot Springs to my base at Fishing Bridge when I noticed a sizable flock of ravens in a meadow at Willow Park, south of the Indian Creek campground. I pulled over and observed the ravens through my binoculars and noticed that they were feeding on the remains of an elk. Where there's a carcass, there are scavengers, and wolves are not above scrounging for their meals. It was just after dawn, so I decided to spend the morning huddled inside a copse of young lodgepole pines about 500 feet from the carcass.

I pulled off the road a fair distance from the grove of trees. After screwing my camera onto my tripod and mounting my 600mm telephoto onto my camera, I hiked up the road and into the trees, where I sat patiently in the shade on a soft mound of pine duff for a couple of hours. The sun was at my back, and the meadow was bathed in soft, early morning light. Beyond the carcass, the lush meadow gave way to a reedy wetland and a beyond that, a low, gravely ridge strewn, like a dinosaur bone yard, with old, sun-bleached timbers formed the horizon. It was a perfect setting. Moreover, I had that carcass all to myself; there wasn't another photographer in sight, and what was better, I wasn't visible from the road. In other words, I would not draw a crowd. In Yellowstone, it hardly gets any better than this!

Around 10:00 AM, what I took for a large German shepherd appeared over the ridge. I was enraged at the thought that some campers in the nearby campground had let their dog loose in violation of park rules, thus spoiling what—even without attracting a wolf—had been a delightful morning. Expressing their contempt, the ravens flew off in various directions, and a couple of entertaining coyotes who had been playing tug of war with a femur also bolted.

But wait, that dog wasn't acting quite right. It was being much too careful, too circumspect in its approach to the carcass. This animal hesitated. It cast furtive glances over its shoulder. It circled the carcass. It was acting . . . like a wild animal! (Understand that I had never seen a wolf in the wild before.) *Hey, that's no German shepherd!*

My heart jumped into my throat, and instantly the roar of blood rushing through my head overwhelmed any other sound. I trained my lens on the wolf and maintained my composition (and my composure) as he slowly, cautiously approached the carcass. A few feet shy of the carcass, he stopped and cast a glance straight at me. Through the lens, I could see his amber eyes and black pupils! I pressed the shutter and the motor drive got off two frames before the wolf turned and resumed its measured advance toward the carcass. He came within biting distance of the rotting bones, fur, and sinew—there was little if any meat remaining—sniffed the putrid meat, and continued loping casually toward the wetland. At the base of the ridge, he cast a final glance in my direction, then bounded over the rocks and timbers as easily as an owl navigates its way among the trees and branches in the forest, and vanished over the crest. No one said wolves aren't picky.

These days wolves inhabit most of the park. Still, your best opportunity for seeing any of these elusive animals is in the Lamar Valley, especially between the Yellowstone Association Institute and the Pebble Creek Campground. You must be in the valley at the crack of dawn or between dinnertime and nightfall. Most mornings and evenings you'll have no trouble knowing where to set up your tripod in hopes that a wolf or pack of wolves will come bounding across your viewfinder; just look for the huddle of "wolfers" at one of the pullouts or forming a leggy sentinel of tripods and lenses atop a low hill just off the road. These are folks

Pronghorn bucks sparring

for whom spotting a wolf—not once but as often as they can—is a religion.

Needless to say, you'll need your longest lens and usually a great deal more. Hence, be prepared to be satisfied with a glimpse, at a great distance, of one of the famous Yellowstone wolves. Remember that most of the outstanding photos of wolves are of captive animals. Don't allow your inability to photograph a wolf, through no lack of preparation on your part, diminish the experience when you finally observe one of these splendid creatures, the personification of wild nature, once again fulfilling its vital role in the Yellowstone wilderness.

As I mentioned earlier, herds of bison and small groups of pronghorn also frequent the Lamar Valley drawn by the lush floodplain and ample water, as well as the open land that makes it difficult for predators to stalk these vulnerable species. Still, the wolves and coy-otes, black bears and grizzlies roam the valley, hoping to ambush or chase down an adult or pick a defenseless calf out of the herd.

Trout Lake (95)

If you're an especially patient photographer and willing to take a gamble, I'll let you in on a little out-of-the-way place that—provided you're prepared to spend the better part of a day in one location—might pay off with a winning wildlife photograph. A bit over a mile west of the Pebble Creek Campground is the trailhead to aptly-named **Trout Lake (95)**. It's roughly a half-mile hike to the lake, up and over a moderately sloping wooded hill. In June the feeder stream leading into the north side of the lake is brimming with spawning **cutthroat trout**. The extremely shallow water—no more than a few inches deep—affords an excellent opportunity to photograph, close up, these stunningly brilliant fish. Any focal length between 50 and 200mm will allow you to frame schools or single fish, respectively. Use a polarizer to remove glare from the water, and choose a sunny day so that the colors of the fish are absolutely dazzling.

Now, if you arrive early or stay through until the late afternoon, and the stream is jam-packed with fish, conceal yourself in the bushes about 100 feet from where the stream enters the lake. Be sure to have a clear line of sight to the mouth of the stream. Where there's food, there are consumers. **Coyotes**, **foxes**, **wolves**, and even **bears** know about this annual food bonanza and will come to avail themselves of the bounty. During my summer in Yellowstone, I heard of an extremely reliable coyote that came to the stream nearly every day to dine on the trout. Alas, by the time I was told about this opportunity, the trout run had waned and, though I staked out the stream for several days, the coyote had moved on.

Thus, if you're inclined, and the trout are running, you may be rewarded with a photo of a coyote, or fox, or . . . well, who knows *what* with a fish in its mouth. But before you set up your tripod, ask the local ranger or other photographers whether they know who's feasting on trout at Trout Lake. If it's a bear, the area will be posted off-limits for your safety.

Another reason for visiting Trout Lake is the family of **otters** living in the lake. These are not your typically reticent otters. This is a family of exhibitionists! They appear almost any time of day, slithering up onto partially submerged snags to pose four or five or six at a time; frolicking in a slick, frenzied knot of playful siblings; and otherwise carrying on for the cameras. A 100mm lens is plenty to capture their antics, but you have to have the reflexes of a fighter pilot to keep up with these restless and energetic animals. Good luck!

Finally, walk along the streams that lead into and out of Trout Lake, and you may spot an **ouzel**, or **dipper**. This remarkable bird was the subject of one of naturalist John Muir's most famous essays, "The Water-Ouzel." On his forays in the Sierras, Muir delighted in the ouzel's charm, defiant tenacity, and, most notably, its aquatic agility. This bird can walk through water, swim through water, and even walk *under* water in search of food, principally aquatic insects that it gleans off the rocks in fast-flowing streams. As Muir put it: "No canyon is too cold for this little bird, none too lonely, provided it be rich in falling water. Find a fall, or cascade, or rushing rapid, anywhere upon a clear stream, and there you will surely find its complementary Ouzel, flitting about in the spray, diving in foaming eddies, whirling like a leaf among beaten foam-bells; ever vigorous and enthusiastic, yet self-contained, and neither seeking nor shunning your company." A plump slate-gray bird about the size of a robin, the ouzel will allow you to sit quietly on the bank of the stream in which it's feeding and—with your camera and 100 to 400mm telephoto lens at hand—enjoy a picnic while photographing it plunging into the foam at the base of a cataract or preening on some half-submerged rock, pausing occasionally to cast a cocky glance at your camera.

I sincerely hope that this guide will add to your enjoyment of Yellowstone National Park—moreover, that it will help you to capture some of the park's natural majesty in photographs that you will be proud to display. It has certainly been a pleasure being your guide.

Feel free to e-mail me from my Web site, Sojourns in Nature, at www.sojournsinnature.com, and let me know whether you found this book useful. I'll also be glad to display some of your best photos in my online gallery.

Once again, may the light be with you.

Suggested Itineraries

I. Mammoth District Hot Springs

6:00–7:00 AM	Look for elk on the terraces, especially on cool mornings. Photograph terraces in morning light.
7:00–9:30 AM	Cruise Swan Lake Flats and Willow Park for moose, coyotes, wolves, and other wildlife.
9:30–11:00 AM	On calm sunny days, photograph reflection of Electric Peak in Swan Lake at Swan Lake Flats.
11:30 AM–12:00 PM	Picnic and photograph yellow-bellied marmots at Sheepeater Cliffs.
12:30–2:30 PM	Explore the upper terraces; photograph hot springs on top of terraces and Orange Spring Mound.
2:30–3:30 PM	Photograph magpies on Old Gardiner Road if sunny, or photograph terraces if cloudy.
4:00–6:30 PM	Explore Blacktail Plateau Drive; look for pronghorn.
6:30–8:00 PM	Look for pronghorn along Old Gardiner Road.

II. Madison and Norris Junctions

6:00–9:00 AM	Choose between steaming landscapes at Norris Geyser basin or elk along the Gibbon River.
9:00 AM	Check for herds of wildlife at the Information Station and Bookstore at Madison Junction.
11:00 AM–1:00 PM	Head to Artists Paint Pots, stopping at Terrace Spring along the way.
1:00–2:30 PM	Visit Norris Geyser Basin to photograph hot springs.
2:45 PM	Visit Roaring Mountain.
3:30 PM	Visit Gibbon Falls.
4:00–6:00 PM	Look for bald eagles along Madison River and forest fire damage between West Entrance and Norris Junction.
6:00 PM–sunset	Cruise for wildlife along between Madison and Canyon junctions.

III. Old Faithful and West Thumb

5:30–7:00 AM	Photograph scenics of Lake Yellowstone and Fishing Cone at sunrise from West Thumb or scenics of Upper Geyser Basin at sunrise.
8:00 AM	Study geyser schedule over breakfast; determine where you will want to be and when to photograph the day's erupting geysers.
9:00 AM	Explore the Old Faithful Inn.
10:00 AM–3:00 PM	Follow the day's geyser schedule to photograph erupting geysers.
12:00 AM–3:00 PM	Photograph hot springs, including Grand Prismatic Spring and Morning Glory Pool and thermophyllic bands at Biscuit and Black Sand basins.
3:00 PM	Visit Fountain Paint Pot Nature Trail.
4:30 PM–sunset	Look for Castle and Grand Geysers to produce rainbows if they erupt in the late afternoon. Riverside Geyser receives golden light at the end of the day.
sunset	End the day at Great Fountain Geyser.

IV. Fishing Bridge District

5:30–7:00 AM	Early-morning scenics and wildlife in Hayden Valley.
7:00 AM	Photograph Dragon's Mouth at Mud Volcano; then return to Hayden Valley.
8:30–10:00 AM	Pelicans swim near shore behind the Fishing Bridge Visitor Center.
10:00 AM	Return to Hayden Valley for more wildlife opportunities.
11:00 AM–1:00 PM	Photograph cutthroat trout from Fishing Bridge.
1:00–3:00 PM	Find mudpots at Sulphur Caldron, and picnic at LeHardy's Rapids.
3:00–5:00 PM	Photograph cutthroat trout and pelicans at LeHardy's Rapids.
5:00–6:00 PM	Look for afternoon scenics of Yellowstone Lake and Absaroka Range at the Yellowstone Lake Hotel.
7:00 PM–sunset	Cruise for grizzly bears along the East Entrance road, and end with sunset at Lake Butte Overlook.

V. Canyon District

5:30–7:30 AM	Look for elk and moose around Canyon Junction.
7:30–9:00 AM	Artist Point for early-morning compositions.
9:00 AM	Rainbow appears on Upper Falls from Uncle Tom's.
9:45–10:00 AM	Rainbow appears on Lower Falls from Artist Point.
11:00 AM–2:00 PM	Look for ground squirrels, bighorn sheep, wildflowers, and landscapes along Mount Washburn Trail.
3:00 PM–sunset	Photograph canyon formations at Inspiration Point, Lookout Point, and from Cascade Overlook Trail.

VI. Tower-Roosevelt and the Lamar Valley

5:00–8:00 AM	Look for wolves in the Lamar Valley.
8:00–10:30 AM	Photograph the rainbow at Tower Fall.
11:00 AM–12:30 PM	Walk the Chittenden Road for mountain bluebirds.
1:00 PM	Visit the petrified tree.
1:30–2:30 PM	Photograph the balsalt columns, and look for bighorn sheep at Calcite Springs Overlook.
3:00–6:00 PM	Photograph otter, trout, and water ouzel at Trout Lake.
6:30 PM–nightfall	Return to the Lamar Valley for wolves.

Technical Specifications

Subject	Nikon FE2	Canon EOS3	Other	Lens	F-stop/shutter speed	Kodak E100G	Kodak E100GX	Kodak E100VS	Fuji Velvia 50	Gitzo G1340 [1]	Gitzo Studex [2]	Handheld	Bogen	Minolta incident	In-camera	Sunny 16 + 2 stops	Other
Bison grazing (p. 1)		•		Canon 300mm f/2.8 L IS USM	1/250" @ f/5.6	•				•				•			
Beehive Geyser and the Firehole River (p. 3)	•			Nikkor 50mm f/1.8 with polarizer	1/125" @ f/8		•					•				•	
Old Faithful steaming at sunrise (p. 4)	•			Nikkor 50mm f/1.8	1/60" @ f/1.8		•					•			•		
Pelican on the Yellowstone River (p. 7)	•			Nikkor 50mm f/1.8	1/125" @ f/1.8		•					•			•		
East fire (pp. 14–15)	•			Nikkor 50mm f/1.8	1/125" @ f/8		•						•		•		
Sunrise on Yellowstone Lake (p. 17)		•		Nikkor 50mm f/1.8, 81A warming filter	1.2" @ f/16.5		•					•			•		
Elk in Yellowstone National Park (p. 16)		•		Canon 300mm f/2.8 L IS USM	1/350" @ F/8	•				•				•			
Fishing Cone at sunrise (p. 19)	•			Nikkor 50mm f/1.8	4" @ f/22		•					•			•		
Grizzly bear (p. 21)		•		Canon 300mm f/2.8 L IS USM	1/350" @ f/2.8	•				•				•			
Bison grazing (p. 24)		•		Canon 300mm f/2.8 L IS USM	1/125" @ f/4	•					•			•			
Roosevelt Arch with rainbow (p. 28)			3	28-135mm zoom at 28mm	1/15" @ f/11						•						
Bighorn ram (p. 29)		•		Canon 300mm f/2.8 [5]	1/180" @ f/4	•									•		
Green algae patterns on Travertine Terrace (p. 31)	•			Nikkor 50mm f/1.8 with polarizer	1/60" @ f/5.6			•			•			•			
New Blue Spring (p. 32)	•			Nikkor 24mm f/2 with polarizer	1/15" @ f/16			•			•			•			
Raven on Orange Spring Mound (p. 33)	•			Nikkor 50mm f/1.8	1/60" @ f/11			•		•							
Black-billed magpie (p. 33)		•		Canon 300mm f/2.8 [6]	1/350" @ f/5.6	•					•			•			
Coyote pair (p. 34)		•		Canon 300mm f/2.8 [6]	1/250" @ f/5.6	•						•		•			
Cool moose (p. 35)		•		Canon 300mm f/2.8 [6]	1/350" @ f/5.6	•					•						
Burnt lodgepole stump (p. 36)	•			Nikkor 24mm f/2	1/125" @ f/8.25			•		•							
Thermophile bands at Norris Geyser (p. 40)	•			Nikkor 50mm f/1.8 with polarizer	1/60" @ f/11.5			•			•			•			
Roaring Mountain (p. 41)	•			Nikkor 50mm f/1.8	1/60" @ f/16	•						•					
Bull Elk in Velvet with Oncoming Storm (p. 43)		•		Canon 300mm f/2.8 [6]	1/90" @ f/5.6	•					•						
Sunrise at West Thumb Geyser Basin (pp. 44–45)	•			Micro-Nikkor 200mm f/4	1/30" @ f/22			•		•							
Big Cone and Yellowstone Lake (p. 46)	•			Nikkor 50mm f/1.8 with polarizer	1/125" @ f/8			•			•						
Fishing Cone and Yellowstone Lake (p. 47)	•			Nikkor 50mm f/1.8 with polarizer	1/125" @ f/8			•			•						
Old Faithful erupting (p. 49)	•			Nikkor 50mm f/1.8 with polarizer	1/125" @ f/8			•				•				•	
Heart Spring and Lion Geyser (p. 51)	•			Nikkor 50mm f/1.8 with polarizer	1/30" @ f/11			•			•					•	
Rainbow over Castle Geyser (pp. 52–53)	•			Nikkor 50mm f/1.8 with polarizer	1/125" @ f/8.5			•			•						
Riverside Geyser (p. 54)	•			Nikkor 50mm f/1.8 with polarizer	1/125" @ f/5.6			•			•				•		
Morning Glory Pool (p. 55)	•			Nikkor 24mm f/2 with polarizer	1/125" @ f/11.5			•			•						
The unique Old Faithful Inn (p. 56)	•			Nikkor 50mm f/1.8	f/4			•				•					
Grand Prismatic Spring (p. 57)	•			Nikkor 50mm f/1.8 with polarizer	1/60" @ f/8			•				•					
Hot Spring on Firehole Lake Drive (p. 58)	•			Nikkor 50mm f/1.8 with polarizer	1/125" @ f/8			•				•				•	
American white pelican on Alum Creek (p. 59)		•		Canon 300mm f/2.8 [6]	1/500" @ f/5.6	•					•			•			
Bison crossing the Yellowstone River (pp. 60–61)		•		Canon 300mm f/2.8 L IS USM	1/125" @ f/2.8	•					•			•			
Bison calves (p. 62)		•		Canon 300mm f/2.8 L IS USM	1/125" @ f/4	•					•			•			
Steam billowing from Dragon's Mouth (p. 63)	•			Nikkor 24mm f/2 with polarizer	1/125" @ f/8.25			•			•						
Mudpot bubble at Sulphur Caldron (p. 64)		•		Canon 300mm f/2.8 [6]	1/500" @ f/5.6	•				•				•			
Yellow-bellied marmots (p. 65)		•		Canon 300mm f/2.8 [6]	1/125" @ f/5.6	•				•							
Grand Tetons from Lake Butte Overlook (pp. 66–67)		•		Canon 300mm f/2.8 [7]	1/250" @ f/5.6	•					•			•			
Grand Canyon of Yellowstone (p. 68)			4	18mm	1/160" @ f/22								•				
Lower Falls with a rainbow (pp. 70–71)	•			Micro-Nikkor 200mm f/4 with polarizer and 81A warming filter	1/125" @ f/5.6			•			•						
Mule deer on Cascade Lake Trail (p. 73)		•		Canon 300mm f/2.8 [6]	1/125" @ f/5.6	•					•			•			
Twilight over Cascade Lake (pp. 74–75)	•			Nikkor 50mm f/1.8, 81A warming filter	1/250" @ f/5.6	•					•			•			
Burn patterns and Mount Washburn (p. 76)	•			Nikkor 50mm f/1.8	1/125" @ f/8.5			•				•					
Bull elk after shedding velvet (p. 77)		•		Canon 300mm f/2.8 [5]	1/125" @ f/4	•					•			•			
Full moon over the Lamar Valley and pronghorn (p. 79)	•			Nikkor 50mm F/2	1/125" @ f/1.8			•			•			•			
A wolf in the Lamar Valley (p. 81)		•		Canon 300mm f/2.8 [6]	1/500" @ f/5.6	•					•			•			
Pronghorn bucks sparring (p. 83)		•		Canon 300mm f/2.8 [6]	1/125" @ f/5.6			•			•			•			

[1] Gitzo G1340 with Wimberley head [2] Gitzo Studex Performance with Bogen 3047 head [3] Canon EOS 10D [4] Canon EOS 20D [5] L IS USM lens, 1.4x teleconverter, [6] L IS USM, 2x teleconverter [7] L IS USM lens, 2x & 1.4x teleconverters [8] Av/multi-segment metering [9] aperture priority, evaluative metering